SURREY

MAXWELL FRASER

SURREY

B. T. Batsford Ltd
London & Sydney

First published 1975

© Maxwell Fraser 1975

ISBN 0 7134 3029 x

Printed and bound in Great Britain by
Richard Clay (The Chaucer Press) Ltd,
Bungay Suffolk
for the publishers B. T. Batsford Ltd,
14 Fitzhardinge Street, London W1H OAH
and 23 Cross Street, Brookvale, NSW 2100, Australia

CONTENTS

ACKNOWLEDGEMENTS

My indebtedness to past historians and other authors, and to the Surrey Archaeological Collections and Records, is acknowledged in the following pages wherever I have quoted from their works.

I have wandered around Surrey so much, and for so many years, that it is impossible to acknowledge individually all the kindness, help and hospitality I have received in the county from ministers, reference librarians, editors of local newspapers, and officials of the County Council, the old Urban District Councils, and the new District Councils.

When everyone has been so helpful, it is difficult to make any distinctions, but in addition to those mentioned in the text, my special thanks are due to Mr Steve Race and Mr Frank Muir, for the loan of books and documents; Messrs Raymond Mander and Joe Mitchenson, of the Mander and Mitchenson Theatre Collection, Sir Adrian Boult, Lady Jeans, Miss B. E. Gregory, Mr Christopher Monk, Mrs D. G. Neville, Mrs J. E. Burridge, Mrs Rosemarie Biggs, Mrs Susan War, Mr Eric C. Baker, Mr Robert Peters, Mr Ronald Toft, and Mr and Mrs A. H. Hinkin.

I am also most grateful to Mrs Mary Hull and Mrs Roger White for so frequently providing transport and good company to the more remote parts of Surrey, and Miss Mary Pearce for reading the proofs.

The author and publishers would like to thank the following for permission to use the photographs in this book: Archie Handford Ltd, plate 3; A. F. Kersting, plates 2, 5, 6, 7, 8, 9, 12, 13, 14, 15, 16, 18, 19, 20; Kenneth Scowen, plates 1, 4; Mrs Olive Smith, plate 11; Spectrum Colour Library, plate 10. Plate 17 is from the publishers' collection.

LIST OF ILLUSTRATIONS

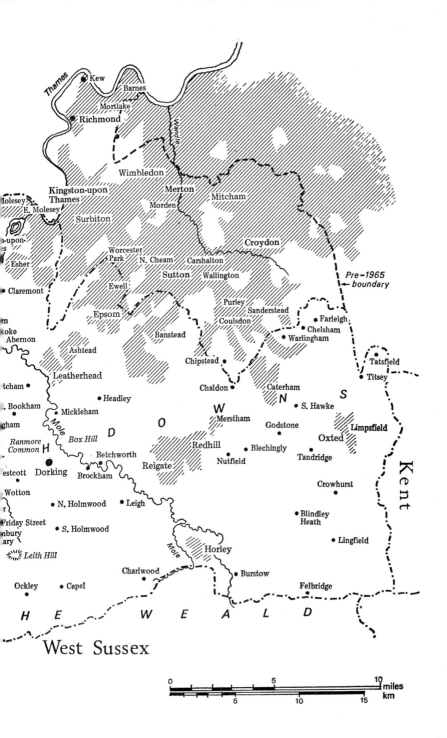

Thames

Kew
Barnes
Mortlake
Richmond

Wimbledon

Kingston-upon Thames
Molesey
E. Molesey
Surbiton

Wandle

Merton
Morden
Mitcham

n-upon-
s
Esher

Claremont

Worcester Park
N. Cheam
Sutton
Ewell

Croydon

Carshalton
Wallington

Pre-1965
boundary

m
.oke
Abernon

Epsom

Purley
Sanderstead
Coulsdon

Farleigh
Chelsham
Warlingham

Ashtead

Banstead

Chipstead

Tatsfield
Titsey

tcham

Leatherhead

Chaldon

Caterham

N   S

. Bookham
gham

Mickleham

Headley

W

Merstham

S. Hawke

Ranmore
Common   H

Mole
Box Hill

O

D

Godstone

Limpsfield
Oxted
Tandridge

Kent

estcott   Dorking
Wotton
r
Friday Street
nbury
ary

Betchworth
Brockham

Reigate

Redhill

Nutfield

Blechingly

Crowhurst

N. Holmwood
Leigh
S. Holmwood

Blindley
Heath

Lingfield

Leith Hill

Mole

Horley

Ockley
Capel

Charlwood

Burstow

Felbridge

H   E   W   E   A   L   D

West Sussex

0   5   10 miles
                            km
      5   10   15

For
Leslie and Louise Wheeler

CHAPTER ONE

Introduction

Surrey is so near to London that many people who have taken only a day trip to one of the county's show-places, or driven through on the way to the coast, seem to think they know all it has to offer. It is true the main roads cross beautiful woodlands and commons, are often in sight of the North Downs and give occasional glimpses of ancient buildings, but Surrey has a gift for hiding its inner life and intimate charm from those who speed by. Few of them realize that there are still large areas devoted to agriculture or horticulture, lanes almost deserted by traffic, and prehistoric trackways where no wheeled traffic can go.

Most of the older Surrey villages turn their backs on the busy main roads, living their own life, and keeping the village green, church, manor-house, inns and cottages hidden away. Even when they have been developed by an influx of new residents from London or other parts of England, they have nearly always succeeded in retaining their individuality, with the newer houses grouped around a railway station, away from the original village centre. Genuine medieval houses still outnumber the mock-Tudor half-timbering, although more scattered and sometimes hard to find. In the urbanized areas along the north-east, bordering on Greater London, where there has been the greatest destruction in the name of 'progress', each place has clung obstinately, even desperately, to some cherished link with the past, and there is frequently a village nucleus hidden away from all but those prepared to take the trouble to seek it out.

The boundaries of Surrey, unlike those of the majority of English counties, do not correspond with the area of some ancient tribe or petty kingdom. Surrey was 'Suthridge', the southern half of a district occupied by the middle Saxons, as Middlesex represented the northern half. Both had come under the rule of the kings of Essex by the sixth century.

The great forest of the Weald, impervious to the tools of pre-historic man, and the sandy north-west region, were uninviting to the earliest settlers. The remains of Iron and Bronze Age settlements have been found scattered over the fertile alluvial soil of the Thames Valley, but it was the high chalk ridge of the North Downs which enabled trackways to run from Stonehenge and the Hampshire coast to the Kentish coast. Prehistoric sites grew up near the trackways, and can be found on the North Downs and a few isolated hills.

The earliest of the roads through Surrey built by the Romans was the Calleva Atrebatum, from London to Silchester and Bath, which crosses the Thames at Staines. Stane Street ran from London to Chichester, and there were other roads from London to the south coast, with linking minor roads. Here and there on the Downs, in the Thames Valley and the Weald, some small patch of iron-bearing, chalk or fertile soil induced a Roman to build a villa, and the later Saxons to make clearings, but archaeologists, historians and philologists have produced many convincing proofs that Surrey was always extremely sparsely inhabited in comparison with the coastal counties, until the influx of wealthy London merchants began under the Tudors.

Surrey saw some decisive battles during the Roman, Saxon and Danish invasions, and by the early tenth century, Guildford and other Surrey towns and villages had been founded, including Kingston upon Thames, which was chosen for the coronation of a succession of Saxon kings. Apart from this, the early history of Surrey is obscure, and even the date when it was Christianized is not known with certainty.

At the time of the Norman Conquest, much of Surrey belonged to Earl Godwin. The Conqueror granted the greater part of Godwin's Surrey lands to his own half-brother, Odo, Bishop of Bayeux, and most of the remainder to Richard de Tonbridge. Later, the de Warennes had vast possessions in the county.

Surrey saw the dawn of English civil liberties at Runnymede, where the barons forced King John to seal the Magna Charta; Surrey labourers joined with those of Sussex, Kent and Essex in the

Peasants' Revolt of 1381; Jack Cade, leader of the 1450 rebellion, may have been a Surrey man by marriage and residence, and the mass of his followers came from Surrey, openly supported by some of the Surrey landowners and townsmen. Surrey favoured the Yorkists in the Wars of the Roses, and the Parliamentarians in the Civil War, and the county had its martyrs, both Roman Catholic and Protestant.

Geologically, Surrey is divided mainly into roughly fan-shaped areas, with the low-lying Thames Valley of London Clay merging on the north-west into the wider Bagshot Beds, which consist chiefly of light sand. The chalk Downs are at their narrowest on the west, where they are barely a mile wide, and spread out to 12 miles on the Kentish border. South of the Downs, a belt of Lower Greensand is at its widest on the Hampshire border, and the Weald Clay extends south to the Sussex border, with a small patch of Hastings Beds in the far south-east. There are also narrow Old Haven, Woolwich and Reading Beds outlining the northern edge of the chalk hills, and equally narrow belts of Gault and Upper Greensand outlining the southern slope of the Downs.

No county in the south-east has a greater diversity of scenery. Even in the Thames Valley there are such famous view-points as Richmond Hill and Cooper's Hill, and various lesser heights, and there are lush meadows and mixed woodlands among the bricks and mortar, merging into the heathlands and fir trees on the Berkshire border. The chalk hills of the North Downs have entirely different vegetation. The Weald has yet another type of scenery, and there are pine-clad hills and valleys in the Hindhead area. Leith Hill is the highest peak in the south-east of England.

Surrey is particularly rich in its flora. It is claimed that out of 1,861 native and naturalized plants in Great Britain, Surrey has no less than 1,081. It has been known since the time of White of Selborne that Surrey has much to interest ornithologists, and the area of Middlesex lying between the Thames and the A4, with its enormous reservoirs, which is now included in Surrey, is also famous among bird-watchers. Game birds are few, but many rare species of smaller birds flourish in the absence of the large birds of prey found in the north of England and Scotland.

Although Surrey has no sea-coast, it has the Thames, so beloved by those who live on its banks. The county affords ample opportunities for freshwater sports, which are supplemented by the sailing and angling on lakes and reservoirs.

Innumerable small streams contribute to the fertility and charm of the county, and have been used to operate water-mills for centuries past, but only three are of special importance—the Wey, which was made navigable as far as Godalming by the Wey Navigation Canal, the Mole, which wanders erratically for 42 miles, usually well away from towns, or even villages, and has no commercial importance at all, and the Wandle, which rises on the Downs above Croydon, and joins the Thames near Wandsworth Bridge. It descends too rapidly to be navigable, except in the lower reaches. The Wandle has always been used as a source of water-power, and its banks are largely urbanized.

People from London and other parts of England have been settling in Surrey in ever-increasing numbers since the Dissolution of the monasteries freed lands for private ownership. The Mores, Onslows, Evelyns, Brays, Howards, Lovelaces and many others are among Surrey's most illustrious families, and some of their descendants are still living on their ancestral lands. It was often the wealth and discriminating taste of these men which brought distinction to Surrey in architecture, and enterprise in agriculture and horticulture, although the name of William Cobbett stands out among them as a Surrey man born and bred who cared passionately for his native county, and for the prosperity of English agriculture.

The later City merchants, who drove in their carriages to their London offices every morning and returned at night, were the forerunners of those who now travel to and fro by rail or road, and they have always been balanced by the Surrey men who went to London to live. Nor must it be forgotten that among those who have chosen to live in Surrey, even if they work in London, are some of the leading musicians, artists, actors and creative writers of today.

In the nineteenth century, it was a Londoner living in Surrey, Sir Robert Hunter, who was one of the founders of the National Trust, which has preserved so many acres of Surrey, as well as in other parts of the country, in their natural beauty.

Londoners have helped to arrest the drift from the country to the town, so evident in many other English counties, and in Wales, for except in some areas along the banks of the Thames, there are few if any of the 'holiday bungalows', empty for the greater part of the year, which have aroused so much resentment elsewhere. Inevitably, some of the newcomers show little or no interest in their new surroundings, but a far larger proportion are generous supporters, with both time and money, of all village activities. They have helped to revitalize many small communities, until there is hardly a village in Surrey without its village cricket team, its choral society and local history society. Many villages also support dramatic and operatic societies and other cultural and sporting activities.

Although it is one of the smallest of English counties, three new theatres have been built in recent years, at Leatherhead, Guildford and Farnham—four, if Croydon's Ashcroft Theatre is included— and there are numerous music festivals, of which those of Leith Hill, Box Hill, Tilford and Haslemere are already famous far beyond the county boundaries. All these have fostered a close-knit community spirit in the towns and villages, and the newcomers are often in the forefront of any fight to protect a local beauty spot or architectural gem.

My love-affair with Surrey began before the Second World War, when I had relatives at Reigate, and made it a centre for exploring East Surrey, and at Churt, a splendid centre for the whole of the south-west. I visited Bisley for the shooting contests when an uncle competed there, and from my own home I constantly cycled and walked the by-ways of the Thames Valley, including that part of Middlesex which is now incorporated in Surrey. I have also rowed, punted, sailed or travelled by motor-launch or steamer along the whole 40 miles of the Thames between Runnymede and Deptford Creek. Since 1972, I have revisited all parts of Surrey, and have noted all too many changes—but have also seen how much remains unchanged in this lovely and lovable county.

With the reorganization of the local authorities in 1974, and the slow progress of new motorways across the county, Surrey has been in a state of flux. The M3, M23 and M25, which were due to open in the Spring of 1974, are still under construction at the time of writing, and some sections are likely to be held up for some time to come, through fierce local opposition.

Hotels change owners—or chefs—too frequently to be recommended safely, and all that can be said is that the range is enormous, both for accommodation, or for lunching and dining—but those who enjoy their afternoon tea are now less well served. Few indeed are the country hotels and restaurants which still serve tea, and the delightful little tea-rooms which were once to be found in almost every village have practically disappeared.

The best way of getting to know Surrey is to leave the highways, as Cobbett advised over 150 years ago. Those whose time is limited will find much to see along the main roads, and a car will enable them to follow the maze of erratically winding lanes—but it is still better to leave the car at some point, and explore on foot. It is also possible to make use of such rural stations as remain or the bus and coach services.

Surrey had no cathedral until Guildford Cathedral was consecrated in 1961. Nor did it have a university until the University of Surrey was given a Royal Charter in 1966. There are only slight remains of such once great abbeys as Chertsey, Newark, Waverley and Merton, but the palaces of the Archbishops of Canterbury at Croydon and Addington—both now in London—survive, and there are many interesting churches, some of Saxon foundation, and some almost untouched since Norman times.

The royal palace of Kew survives, but there is little to be seen of Richmond Palace, and only the sites of Nonsuch, Oatlands, Guildford and Woking palaces, but the county has often given refuge to exiled foreign royalty—especially at Claremont, but also in other parts of the county, right down to our own day. Surrey's castles played little part in national events. There are Norman mottes at Walton-on-the-Hill, Abinger and Blechingly; castles at Guildford and Farnham, and rather scanty remains at Reigate and Sterborough or Starborough, near Lingfield.

The lack of castle ruins is compensated for by the splendid mansions, many Georgian houses, and some of the most perfect medieval timber-framed brick houses to be seen anywhere in England. Most of these have glorious gardens, so many of which are open to the

1 (opposite above) *Richmond Bridge*

2 (opposite below) *Maids of Honour Row, Richmond*

public from time to time that it has not been possible to mention more than a few. Those who are interested should consult the booklets issued by the National Gardens Scheme Committee and the Gardeners' Sunday Organization.

Surrey has been a county of great gardeners since the days of Sir Francis Carew of Bedlington and John Evelyn of Sayes Court and Wotton. If it has lost Kew Gardens to Greater London, it still has Wisley, the Savill Garden and Valley Gardens, and Winkworth Arboretum. In our own time, Gertrude Jekyll is unquestionably the greatest of women writers on horticulture, and Surrey had three other women—Mrs C. W. Earle, Eleanour Sinclair Rohde, and Marion Cran—who in their very different ways, did much to popularize gardening by their writings and example.

There are a number of old water-mills and windmills, and some of the best—as well as the worst!—Victorian and twentieth-century architecture. Such towns as Guildford, Farnham, Godalming and Haslemere are an especial delight, but the villages and the remote farmhouses are Surrey's greatest charm.

3 (opposite) *Wrencote, in the High Street, Croydon*

CHAPTER TWO

Surrey in Greater London

Less than a century ago all the London boroughs from Deptford Creek to Putney were a part of Surrey. When the Act of 1888 transferred 25,798 acres of the north-east of Surrey to the metropolis, it not only deprived the county of its most important outlet to the sea, but of places so bound up with Surrey's history that to have a full understanding of the part played by Surrey in national affairs it is necessary to glance, however briefly, at some of this background.

The great Surrey Docks still bear the county name, although it is planned to fill them in and develop them with housing and factories in the course of time. The Oval at Kennington is the home of Surrey's County Cricket Club, and every devotee of the Oxford and Cambridge Boat Race knows the advantages of winning the toss, and taking the route 'along the Surrey side'.

Among the famous places in this densely populated area are Lambeth Palace, seat of the Archbishops of Canterbury; St Thomas's Hospital; the site of the great Bermondsey Abbey; and the Royal Dockyards at Deptford and Rotherhithe, set on the tidal estuary of the Thames. It was at Deptford that Queen Bess knighted Sir Francis Drake on his return from his voyage around the world; the Pilgrim Fathers gathered before their embarkation to the New World; Peter the Great, Czar of Russia, worked as a carpenter; and General Oglethorpe and his settlers set sail for Georgia. Greenland Whalers and many other adventurers made it their port.

The conscientious Pepys was a frequent visitor to Deptford on his naval duties, and spent his retirement at Clapham, where he died in 1703. His friend and fellow diarist, John Evelyn, made his home at Sayes Court for over 40 years, discovered the young Grinling Gibbons, and set him on the road to fame

Southwark had the Tabard Inn where the Canterbury pilgrims gathered before the final stage of their journey to Canterbury Cathedral; the Globe, Hope and Rose playhouses, where the plays of Shakespeare, Marlowe, Massinger, and Beaumont and Fletcher were first produced; and the Marshalsea Prison and other places associated with scenes and characters in the novels of Charles Dickens. It still has the galleried George Inn where Mr Pickwick met the immortal Sam Weller. William Emerson, born in the parish in 1483, is said to have been an ancestor of Ralph Waldo Emerson, the American poet and essayist, and John Harvard, after whom Harvard University, Massachusetts, is named, was born in Southwark in 1607. Both are commemorated in the cathedral.

Vauxhall had its Gardens, Battersea its famous enamels, and Putney its Roehampton. Other boroughs south of the Thames-side area also contributed to Surrey's Roll of Honour, notably Dulwich with its famous College and Art Gallery, and Streatham, where Dr Johnson, Mrs Thrale, Fanny Burney and other members of the Johnson Circle foregathered—but the list is too long to be given here, unfortunately.

As if the loss to Surrey of this brilliant background was not enough, in 1965 London took over another slice of the county. The local authorities dutifully styled themselves London boroughs, but the citizens stubbornly refused to relinquish their ties with Surrey— and who shall blame them? It is unthinkable that the contribution to Surrey of such places as Richmond, Kew, Kingston, Wimbledon, Sutton, Croydon, Mitcham, Morden and Merton should be forgotten. There is but little compensation in the addition of a small area of Middlesex, north of the Thames, which is equally reluctant to forsake its ties with Middlesex and regard itself as part of Surrey.

It is true that even before the 1939–45 war, a great tide of monotonous suburban houses had swamped much of the area, and the process has speeded up in the last 20 years, but there are still places where it is possible to walk among country sights and scenes, as the *Country Walks* booklets issued by London Transport show. The Green Belt policy has saved these former Surrey boroughs from complete loss of identity. Usually backed by the more enlightened borough councils, and by the efforts of Residents' Associations and the

National Trust, large areas of commons and parks have been preserved, and even some of the older houses.

Cricketers' Green at Old Mitcham, still has cricketers carrying on a long tradition. The first recorded match there was between the Gentlemen of London and the Gentlemen of Mitcham in 1730, and it is believed cricket was played there long before this date. A fair formerly held on the green is now held annually on King's Piece, where the roundabouts and side-shows cover nearly 17 acres. It is one of the oldest and largest in or near London.

There are some old inns and Georgian houses from the days when it was a fashionable London suburb, and scent works are a reminder of the lavender farms for which Mitcham was once so famous, and which supplied the London street-sellers with their bunches of 'Sweet Lavender'.

Morden has the brick church of St Lawrence, dating from 1636—a rare period in church building, which adds to its interest. Seventeenth-century Morden Hall; the late Georgian Morden Grange; Morden Park House with a fragment of crinkle-crankle wall in the stable yard, and the beautiful Ravensbury Park beside the River Wandle survive, but many homes of distinguished Londoners have vanished, including that of Captain Alexander Maconochie, one of the founders of the Royal Geographical Society.

Merton's losses have been lamentable. The pattern was set by Henry VIII, who took the stones of Merton Priory to build his palace of Nonsuch. Twentieth-century Merton has obliterated every trace of Nelson's beloved home, and even William Morris's workshops beside the River Wandle have disappeared. Merton Priory, founded in 1114, once owned wide lands, and it was in the priory that the Statute of Merton was enacted in 1236. It was the most ancient body of laws after Magna Charta. Walter de Merton, who founded Merton College, Oxford, in 1264 may have been born at Merton, and probably received his education in the priory. All that remains today is a gateway and some walling, half-hidden by factories, and a handsome doorway re-erected in the churchyard of the parish church. The church itself, although largely rebuilt, also has a Norman doorway and other attractive details from the earlier church on the site.

Wimbledon's vast common has a much-photographed windmill

and the so-called Caesar's Camp, which is an Iron Age hill fort, but its greatest fame is based on the courts of the All-England Croquet and Lawn Tennis Club, on which the International Lawn Tennis Championships are played.

Wimbledon House, built for Sir Thomas Cecil, first Earl of Exeter and son of Lord Burghley, was enlarged by Inigo Jones for Queen Henrietta Maria, but was demolished in the eighteenth century. Sarah, Duchess of Marlborough, built a more fashionable house, which was burned down later in the same century. Even its successor has vanished, but part of the park is now used for the Royal Wimbledon Championship Golf Course.

Croydon and Sutton have engulfed neighbouring villages, and much of beauty and interest has inevitably been destroyed, especially during the air-raids of 1940–45, when Croydon, in particular, suffered severely.

At first sight, Croydon appears to be an entirely post-war development. Even those who know it has had over a thousand years of recorded history—it celebrated its millennium in 1960—gain the impression that everything has been sacrificed to the modern craze for tower-block offices and flats, shopping precincts and other adjuncts of modern town planning, and react accordingly. Opinions vary from unqualified praise to a lament for things past and gone for ever.

Civic pride is centred especially on the Fairfield Halls opened in 1962, incorporating a concert hall which has become world-famous, the successful Ashcroft Theatre named after Dame Peggy Ashcroft, who was born in Croydon, and the Arnhem Gallery.

The Whitgift Centre, a million-pound shopping precinct, occupies eleven acres on the original site of the Whitgift School founded by Archbishop Whitgift. The parish church of St John the Baptist (the largest in Surrey) was rebuilt in 1870 after a fire which destroyed all but the fifteenth-century tower and two-storied south porch. With the help of drawings and sketches made by John Corbet Anderson before the fire, Sir Gilbert Scott was able to restore the church and the tomb of Archbishop Whitgift to the original design.

Five other Archbishops of Canterbury were buried there, including Archbishop Sheldon, founder of the Sheldonian Theatre at Oxford who died in 1677. Among others buried there are Thomas Hutchinson, the last royal governor of Massachusetts, and John Singleton Copley, the American-born artist who was the father of John Singleton Copley the Younger, afterwards Lord Lyndhurst, Lord Chancellor of England.

The Archbishops had their country house in Croydon from the time of the Conquest until 1780, when they removed to Addington Palace, now also within the Croydon boundary. The medieval palace survives in Old Palace Road, in spite of many later changes of usage. It is now a school. It has a splendid hall with an open-timber roof dating from the mid-fifteenth century, and a twelfth-century undercroft.

The lovely Whitgift Hospital in North End, built in 1596 to provide homes for 40 infirm old people from the parishes of Croydon and Lambeth, is still used as an almshouse today. There are some Georgian town houses, chiefly down by the River Wandle, and a number of old shops, inns and cottages in Old Town. No. 46 Southend, a timber-framed house with an overhanging upper storey, claims to be the oldest shop in Croydon, and Wrencote, in the High Street, south of the flyover, is the town's finest eighteenth-century house. The Waddon Caves in Alton Road were excavated in 1902, and revealed Neolithic and Iron-Age relics, suggesting the site was occupied until the fifth century AD.

Samuel Coleridge Taylor, the composer praised by Elgar and Sullivan as 'the cleverest fellow among the younger men' lived and worked in Croydon as a teacher and conductor. He died in 1912 at the age of 37, and is buried in Bandon Hill cemetery, Wallington. He is best remembered by the older generation for his *Hiawatha* trilogy, which was produced at the Albert Hall annually from 1922 to 1939 (excepting 1926, during the General Strike), and was such an immense success that it set every amateur baritone singing *Onaway, Awake Beloved* on every possible occasion.

Ruskin's maternal grandmother was the landlady of the old King's Head, since demolished, and he spent many happy hours with his relations there during his boyhood. Conan Doyle set several Sherlock Holmes stories in the area.

Croydon made railway history in 1801, with the first Act for a public railway, in the sense in which that term is understood today, as distinct from those which were used by collieries and ironworks. The Surrey Iron Railway ran from the Thames at Wandsworth to Croydon, with a branch to some mills on the River Wandle. The nine and a half miles of track were taken up in 1846, but it had established the principle of a general public railway, and all early railway legislation was framed on the same lines.

The Croydon Aerodrome, established in 1915 to provide air defence for London, became a civil airport for the metropolis in 1920, and by 1928 was the most modern airport in the world. It was used by the Royal Air Force in the 1939–45 war, and was frequently the target for enemy attack. It remained the main airport for London until development in air traffic necessitated the removal to Heathrow. The aerodrome finally closed in 1959, and part of the site has been built over.

Addington Palace, a beautiful house built in 1773 by Robert Mylne for Barlow Trecothick, a Lord Mayor of London, was owned by the Archbishops of Canterbury from 1808 to 1896. It is now owned by the Croydon Council and has been let to the Royal School of Church Music. Founded in 1927 as the School of English Church Music, it was granted a royal charter in 1945, and moved to Addington Palace in 1954. Today it has over 8,000 affiliated members, chiefly choirs and choral groups ranging from those of great cathedrals to small parish churches and schools. It has done wonderful work in fostering and stimulating the study of church music, of which it has a splendid collection. It also has a publishing department which has become one of the greatest publishing houses of church music in the world, providing books, music lists and church music throughout this country and the Commonwealth.

The palace is backed by the Addington Hills and overlooks the old village with its church. St Mary's has a Norman chancel with original windows, a thirteenth-century south arcade and a tower partly rebuilt in brick in the eighteenth century. There are several brasses and seventeenth- and eighteenth-century monuments. An ornate cross in the churchyard commemorates Archbishop Tait, who died in 1882, and five other nineteenth-century archbishops who are buried there.

Shirley, on Croydon's eastern border, has a famous windmill immediately behind the John Ruskin Grammar School. The tarred brick mill-tower dates from the early nineteenth century, and is now used as a changing room by the school. Ruskin's parents are buried in the churchyard of the Victorian church of St John the Evangelist, with an epitaph composed by their son. Sir William Purdie Treloar, a famous carpet merchant, who founded the Lord Mayor Treloar Hospital at Alton, Hampshire, was buried in the church in 1925.

There are groves of silver birch and huge oak trees on the Shirley Hills, and a viewing platform 600 feet above sea level, presented to Croydon during the millenary celebrations.

Addiscombe Place was used by the East India Company as the main training centre for its officers between 1809 and 1861, but was demolished when a housing estate was laid out there in the 1860s. The celebrated Victorian hostess, Lady Ashburton, entertained Tennyson, Carlyle, Longfellow and other literary celebrities at Addiscombe House, which has been demolished. Addiscombe also had associations with Thackeray.

Sir Arthur Conan Doyle lived at 10 Tenison Place, South Norwood, which is marked by a GLC plaque, Samuel Coleridge Taylor lived at 10 Upper Grove, and Charles Brock, the fireworks manufacturer, also lived there.

Coulsdon Old Church, dating from the thirteenth century, is set beside a large green. It has a curious acrostic inscription to Grace Rowed, who died in 1631.

Although Purley appears in documents as early as the twelfth century, when it was spelled 'Pirle' or 'Pirles', it remained little more than a name. Its largest house, Purleybury, was occupied in the eighteenth century by William Tooke, who persuaded John Horne to add the name of Tooke to his own, after he had fought an Enclosure Act, which saved William's Purley property. John Horne Tooke, although in holy orders, was a notorious political agitator.

As late as 1870, there were still only about 140 houses in Purley, but it has developed considerably since then.

Selsdon Woods are now a bird sanctuary, and there are more woodlands on the Addington Hills and Croham Hurst, with Celtic fields on Farthing Down, and Saxon barrows above Coulsdon. The rural scene at Bradmore Green, with an eighteenth-century farm and a brick barn near the church, is under a Conservation Order.

Sanderstead, south-east of Croydon, extends to the Surrey border near Warlingham. Sanderstead is set among the wooded hills and lush fields of the North Downs. The church, mainly of thirteenth- and fourteenth-century work, was damaged by a bomb in the 1939–45 war, but has interesting brasses and monuments. Near the churchyard gate is the grave of Sir Francis Head, author and colonial administrator, who died in 1876. He was descended from Dr Ferdinando Mendoza, the physician of Queen Catherine of Braganza. *Rough Notes of Journeys in the Pampas and the Andes* describes his journeys in South America, and among his many other books, *Stokers and Pokers*, published in 1849, gives a vivid account of the difficulties in constructing and maintaining a railway. There is a splendid panoramic view from the cemetery, which lies on the opposite side of the road from the church.

Sanderstead Court was bombed in 1944, and has been replaced by terraced houses. Only the north wing survives, as the Selsdon Park Golf Club house.

Sutton, west of Croydon, began to grow when one of the first turnpike roads was constructed in 1755 from London to Brighton. The old Cock Inn became an important coaching stage, and the town itself a social centre with many great houses in the neighbourhood. Sutton has been less careful of its old buildings than Croydon. The original Cock Inn was demolished in 1961, and only the inn sign remains, above a signpost at the crossroads.

The church of St Nicholas was rebuilt in 1862, and its only feature of interest is an eighteenth-century mausoleum of the Gibson family of London. In 1793, Elizabeth Gibson left money for the vicar and churchwardens to open the gate of the mausoleum, and inspect the coffins. This is still done annually at 6 p.m. on 12 August.

Among the villages now included in the borough boundary is Beddington, on the east, where cattle graze in the fields beside the River Wandle as it flows through Beddington Park, once the home of the Carews, who came from Pembrokeshire to Beddington in 1350. Fuller says Sir Nicholas Carew 'was a jolly gentleman, fit for the favour of King Henry the Eighth, who loved active spirits, as

27

could keep pace with him in all his achievements, and made him knight of the Garter and master of his horse'. Unfortunately, when the King spoke rudely to him, Sir Nicholas returned an answer 'rather true than discreet', and so offended the King that Sir Nicholas 'fell from the top of his favour to the bottom of his displeasure, and was bruised to death thereby'. He was beheaded in 1539 on a trumped-up charge of treason, and the king took possession of his estates.

Mary Tudor restored the estates to his son, Sir Francis, who wisely kept away from the Court and lived quietly at Beddington, cultivating his garden. Sir Francis was a skilful horticulturalist, and built an orangery which is said to have been the first in England in which oranges were grown successfully. According to tradition, the seeds were given to him by Sir Walter Raleigh, who had married Carew's niece, Bessie Throckmorton, but more probably he brought the seed himself from Naples. His ingenious devices are described by Sir Hugh Platt in *The Garden of Eden*.

Sir Francis died a bachelor, and left Beddington to his nephew, Nicholas Throckmorton, on condition he changed his name to Carew. His sister Bessie loved Beddington, and there is a tradition that the body of her husband, Sir Walter Raleigh, is buried in Beddington church, and not in St Margaret's, Westminster.

The last two Carews were not direct descendants. Admiral Sir Benjamin Hallowell, who was born in Canada, inherited it from a cousin, on condition he adopted the name and arms of Carew. He was a distinguished sailor and served under Nelson at Cape St Vincent and the Nile, but his son, Captain Charles Carew, was a spendthrift, and in 1859 the estate which had been held by Carews for over 500 years had to be sold to pay his debts. It is now the Carew Manor Special School, administered by the Borough of Sutton.

A fire in 1865 destroyed the greater part of the house, but the great hall, dating back to 1530, was saved. An eighteenth-century brick dovecot, and a long brick wall of an orangery built on the site where Sir Francis cultivated his oranges, also survive, and now are so jealously protected that public opinion caused the route of the proposed M23 to be diverted to prevent the destruction of the wall.

St Mary's Church, near the manor-house, has masonry dating

back to the eleventh century, with additions made in 1390, when Sir Nicholas Carew left money for the purpose in his will. The Carew Chapel has a splendid array of brasses to the Carews from 1432 onwards, and an alabaster effigy of Sir Francis Carew, who died in 1611. There is also a curious punning epitaph on a steward to Sir Nicholas Carew, who died in 1533.

Ruskin described Carshalton in *The Crown of Wild Olives* in 1870, as sadly declined from its appearance 20 years before, when 'there was no lovelier piece of Lowland scenery in South England . . .'. Ruskin reclaimed the springs, and today the ponds are carefully protected, and the centre of Carshalton is again a delightful place. All Saints, above the High Street and the smaller pond, was extended in the nineteenth century, but has medieval walls, and monuments to the Gaynesfords, Scarwens and others, including an inscription to William Quelche, who as vicar burned incense there even during the Commonwealth until his death in 1654.

Admiral Sir Edward Whitaker, who took part in the capture of Gibraltar in 1704, is buried in the churchyard, but his grave is unmarked, the stone having been lost when the church was enlarged.

Carshalton House, built between 1696 and 1713, was sold to Dr Radcliffe, founder of the Radcliffe Library at Oxford, and two years later to Sir John Fellowes, one of the directors of the South Sea Bubble. It passed some 14 years later to Philip Yorke, afterwards Earl of Hardwicke. The huge brick house has some interesting interior decorations, including an overmantel carved in the Grinling Gibbons tradition. It is now a convent.

'The Oaks', which gave its name to one of the principal races of Derby Week, stood a mile and a half south of Carshalton. It was demolished in 1957.

An Iron-Age fort, and Roman and medieval sherds found on the banks of the River Wandle, suggest there has been a settlement at Wallington since the earliest times, but it was never more than a hamlet until the Victorian era. The library, delightfully situated in a garden, has a children's section with the unusual attraction of a Noah's Ark with over 400 animals.

Cheam has a Victorian church, but preserves the chancel of the older church in the churchyard. It is now known as the Lumley Chapel, and has tombs and the pedigree of 16 generations of the Lumleys, and brasses dating back to 1390, including one to John Yarde, who died in 1449, and his wife, with figures less than seven inches in length.

Although the greater part of Cheam is suburban, it has a village atmosphere in the neighbourhood of the church, where the eighteenth-century brick Rectory faces Whitehall, a timber-framed house of about 1500. Nearby are a number of sixteenth-century and early Georgian houses and cottages.

Four of the rectors of Cheam became bishops, the last of whom was John Hackett, who was once ordered at the point of a Roundhead's pistol to stop the service in Cheam church, but retorted he would do what became him as a priest, and the soldier must do what became him as a soldier—and was left alone.

Worcester Park owes its name to the Earl of Worcester who was appointed Keeper of the Great Park of Nonsuch. It was sold in 1865 for housing development, which covers the whole area right up to and over the Surrey border in the north of Ewell.

H. G. Wells lived at Worcester Park from 1896, when he was first married, until 1900.

All the Thames-side resorts from Barnes to Surbiton were also incorporated into Greater London in 1965. Barnes is the most north-easterly of the old boroughs welded into the new borough of Richmond, which has a river frontage on the Surrey side of some 13 miles of the best scenery of the tidal reaches.

Barnes is all too successful in hiding its attractive groups of Georgian and early Victorian houses from travellers by rail or main road, and after Barn Elms the river view is blocked by huge reservoirs until two miles beyond Hammersmith Bridge, when a number of delightful Georgian houses survive in Barnes Terrace. Even this view is rather marred by the Barnes Railway Bridge, which cuts across the centre of the terrace.

Barn Elms, once owned by Sir Francis Walsingham, Secretary of State to Elizabeth I from 1579 until his death in 1590, was later the summer meeting place of the Kit-Cat Club, whose 30 Whig members bound themselves to support the Protestant succession. Sir Godfrey

Kneller's portraits of the members, who included Steele, Addison, Pope, Dryden and the first Duke of Marlborough, are now in the National Portrait Gallery.

It was at Barn Elms that George Villiers, second Duke of Buckingham, fought his notorious duel in 1668 with the Earl of Shrewsbury. The Countess, disguised as a page, held her lover's horse and fled with the duke as her husband lay dying. Barn Elms later became the Ranelagh Polo Club. The mansion was demolished in 1954, and the grounds are now used as playing fields by local schools. Only an ornamental pond, and an ice-house on a small mound, survive to tell of the glories of the old house.

The parish church of St Mary's has some of the thirteenth-century fabric, an ornamental wall painting, and two brasses, one of Sir Richard Hoare of Barn Elms, who died in 1787, and the other in memory of two young girls of the Wylde family 'which dyed virgyns' in 1508.

Near the church are some attractive Georgian houses, including The Homestead, and the Old Rectory, now known as Strawberry House. The Grange, the Convent of the Sacred Heart and some weather-boarded houses overlook Barnes Common. Milbourne House has an eighteenth-century exterior and a Jacobean interior. The modern buildings to which St Paul's School removed in 1968 are in Lonsdale Road.

Industry at Mortlake was once concentrated on its famous Tapestry Works, and it is distinctly unfortunate that its industry is now centred on its huge and hideous brewery.

The Tapestry Works flourished from 1619 until 1703, reaching their heyday in the reign of Charles I. There is a tablet commemorating the works in a wall of the passage opposite the parish church, and in the church itself is an example of the tapestry made there, hanging behind the vicar's stall. The church is mainly Victorian and Edwardian, with a tower dating from the fifteenth century. Monuments from the older church include a relief by Westmacott and memorials to Sir Philip Francis (1740–1818), one of those credited with being the author of *The Letters of Junius*, and to Henry Addington, Viscount Sidmouth, Prime Minister 1801–4, who is buried in the churchyard.

There is an extraordinary memorial in the Roman Catholic cemetery in North Worple Way to Sir Richard Burton, the explorer and translator of *The Arabian Nights*, and his wife Isabella, who are buried under a full-size stone tent, decorated with crescents and stars, with a crucifix above its entrance.

Thomas Cromwell, the Secretary of State to Henry VIII who was so zealous in the suppression of the monasteries, lived in the manor-house, which has been demolished.

Another famous resident of Mortlake was the astrologer Dr John Dee, who was once prosecuted by the Star Chamber on a charge of magic, but lived to be Chancellor of St Paul's and a favourite of Elizabeth I, who frequently visited him at Mortlake.

West Hall, which dates from the seventeenth century, overlooks the river near the Kew boundary, and in the High Street unimpressive modern flats contrast with attractive Georgian houses. No. 123, with its garden, was painted by Turner. The painting is now in the Frick Collection, New York. The Coach House, in Fitzgerald Avenue, south of the railway, is a 'folly' incorporating seventeenth-century work, and at East Sheen there is the Hare and Hounds Inn dating from about 1760, and some Georgian houses surrounded by much undistinguished modern development.

As all the rowing world knows, the Oxford and Cambridge Boat Race ends at Mortlake, at the Ship Inn, just short of Chiswick Bridge. The boat house where the crews go ashore is on the farther side of the bridge, on the north bank of the river.

Kew Palace, down by the river, is the smallest of the royal palaces formerly at Kew. It was originally built in 1631 in the Dutch style, for a London merchant of Dutch extraction, and is also known as the Dutch House. It was considerably altered in the eighteenth century, when it was the home of various members of the royal family. It became the residence of George III in 1802, but after Queen Charlotte's death in 1818 fell into disuse. It is now in the care of the Department of the Environment, and has much handsome eighteenth-century furniture and many souvenirs of George III and his family. It is open to the public from April to September.

The White House, which stood south-east of the Dutch House, was the home of Frederick, Prince of Wales, in 1722. His widow,

Augusta, Dowager Princess of Wales, laid out the nucleus of Kew Gardens. The site of the White House is marked by a sundial.

St Anne's Church is very effectively set beside the triangular green. The nave and chancel date from the early eighteenth century, with some curious extensions and additions, and numerous interesting monuments. The mausoleum at the east end was added in 1850 for the Duke and Duchess of Cambridge. Sir William Hooker, Director of the Botanical Gardens from 1841 to 1865, and author of a standard work on ferns, is commemorated by a Wedgwood medallion with panels of ferns. His son, Sir Joseph Hooker, who succeeded his father as Director, died in 1911, and is commemorated by ceramic panels of plants. There is a portrait medallion by Westmacott Junior, framed in flowers, to Francis Bauer, a botanical draughtsman, who died in 1840, and a memorial to Lady Capel, who died in 1721, who with her husband, Sir Henry Capel, planted the Capel Gardens which were so highly praised by John Evelyn, and are now incorporated in Kew Gardens.

Among the many distinguished people buried in the churchyard are George Engleheart, the miniaturist, a native of Kew, who was appointed royal miniature painter in 1790; Joshua Kirby, father of Sarah Trimmer, whose children's books were praised by Dr Johnson; John Dodd, the most famous of all English makers of bows for violins and 'cellos in the eighteenth century; Johann Zoffany; Gainsborough and William Aiton, who was appointed to manage the botanic garden at Kew in 1759. In 1789 he published the *Hortus Kewensis, Being a Catalogue of the Plants Cultivated in the Royal Garden of Kew*, which is of historical value for the care with which the dates of introduction of 5,600 species enumerated were ascertained.

William Turner, Dean of Wells, physician and botanist, who spent much of his life on the Continent to avoid religious persecution, had a house and garden at Kew during the short reign of Edward VI. His *Herbal* marked the beginning of scientific botany in England.

Among the Georgian houses around the tree-shaded green, is the Herbarium, which was for many years the home of Queen Victoria's uncle Ernest, Duke of Cumberland, afterwards King of Hanover. Cambridge Cottage was the home of another uncle, Adolphus

Frederick, Duke of Cambridge, and of his son and successor, Prince George.

Cricket has been played on the green for over 200 years. The *London Post* reported on 16 July 1737 a match between Frederick, Prince of Wales, and 10 gentlemen, and the Duke of Marlborough and 10 other noblemen and gentlemen, which was won by the Prince's team.

The gardens laid out by Princess Augusta with the advice of William Aiton were extended by her son, George III, who employed Sir William Chambers and Capability Brown to plan the layout. Much of their work survives today in the Royal Botanical Gardens.

There is a gay little ballad with words by Alfred Noyes, set to music by Graham Peel, which urges *Go Down to Kew in Lilac Time*, but Kew Gardens are a refreshment to the spirit at any time of the year—even in the depths of winter, when the branches of the deciduous trees make patterns against the sky, and the hot-houses offer an exotic refuge from cold winds.

These world-famous Botanical Gardens, covering 300 acres, are a supreme example of the possibility of combining practical research work of the most diverse kinds, with a loveliness which draws Londoners and tourists like a magnet. Not only is there a living collection of some 40,000 different plant species and varieties, but ever since its foundation it has been devoted to scientific and practical purposes, collecting reserves of vanishing plants, introducing bread-fruit and quinine to the former British Empire, now the Commonwealth, and helping to promote the production of cocoa, limes, bananas, cloves, camphor, sisal hemp and many other products which today are taken for granted. The Director now has a staff of some 150 botanists, and one of their aims is to encourage the production of sufficient food crops to sustain the ever-expanding population of the world.

Chief among the landmarks of the Gardens is the Chinese Pagoda, a delightfully odd example of chinoiserie, 163 feet high, which was built by Sir William Chambers purely for decoration. The flagstaff on Victory Hill is a pole made out of a single Douglas fir, felled in 1959, when the tree was about 370 years old, and presented to the Gardens by the Government of British Columbia. The little hill on

34

4 (opposite) *The village pond and White Hart inn, Godstone*

which it stands commands an enchanting vista across the Thames to Syon House.

Among other buildings in the Gardens are the Orangery, built by William Chambers in 1761; the great Palm House, a triumph of nineteenth-century glass-work; a Museum of Economic Botany; a Wood Museum; and the Marianne North Gallery, which has an outstanding collection of over 800 flower paintings by Marianne North. After her father Frederick North, MP for Hastings, died in 1869, Marianne devoted her life to travelling in every part of the world to paint flowers. She not only gave her paintings to Kew, but built the gallery at her own expense, and supervised the arrangement of them before her death in 1890.

Under its original name of Sheen (or Shene), the 'beautiful place', Richmond dates back to Saxon times, and as early as the reign of Henry I belonged to the Crown. After his triumphant career as conqueror of the French, Edward III died his inglorious death in what was little more than a manor-house. Richard II enlarged it for his adored young wife, Anne of Bohemia—and destroyed it after her early death. Henry V restored and enlarged it, and Henry VII rebuilt it on a grander scale after a fire, and renamed it the Palace of Richmond. Both he and Elizabeth I died there—the Queen very dramatically. It is said that near the gatehouse in Old Palace Yard the phantom footsteps can be heard of the messenger who carried Elizabeth's ring, which had been thrown to him from a window as proof of her death, to James VI of Scotland and I of England, riding the 400 miles to Edinburgh in 62 hours.

The palace was dismantled in the Commonwealth, but was largely rebuilt at the Restoration, and remained a royal residence until the Revolution of 1689. It gradually became ruinous, and all that remains is a gateway of Tudor brick, and two ranges of buildings, one of which is in Wardrobe Court.

Among numerous paintings of the old palace are one attributed to Vinkboons (1578–1627), now in the Fitzwilliam Museum, drawings by Wyngaerde of 1562, in the Bodleian Library, and Hollar's engraving of 1638.

Between Richmond Palace, Kew Gardens and the Thames is the Old Deer Park, used by the kings of England for hunting, and now

5 (opposite above) *Monument to 1st Lord Cobham, Lingfield Church*

6 (opposite below) *Monument to Sarah Vincent, Stoke D'Abernon Church*

largely given over to the public for all kinds of sports. It is the home of the London Welsh Rugby Club, among others. The Kew Observatory, built by Sir William Chambers in 1760 for observation of the transit of Venus, is in the Old Deer Park. It is now used as a weather station for the Air Ministry's Meteorological Office.

So small was Richmond, in spite of its royal associations and the famous men drawn there by the proximity of the Court, that it did not become a borough until 1890, and the majority of the older houses are in close proximity around Richmond Green, or on Richmond Hill.

Among the beautiful houses on or near the Green are Old Friars and Old Palace Place, both of which date from 1687; Asgill House, overlooking the river, built by Sir Robert Taylor in 1758 for Charles Asgill, a former Lord Mayor of London; and Trumpeters' House, built in 1701 for Richard Hill, husband of Queen Anne's favourite, 'Mrs Masham'. In later times it was occupied by Prince Metternich, and by Marconi.

Richmond is particularly fortunate in the number of elegant terraced houses which survive, including Old Palace Terrace, The Wardrobe and the best-known of all, Maids of Honour Row, built in 1724 for the maids of honour attending the Princess of Wales, who was then living at Richmond Lodge.

John James Heidegger, who lived at No. 4, is said to have been the ugliest man of his time, and was caricatured by Hogarth, and by Fielding as 'Count Ugly' in *The Pleasures of the Town*. Heidegger was manager of the King's Theatre, Haymarket, for many years, where he was in partnership with Handel for part of the time. Heidegger employed his principal scene-painter, Antonio Joli, to decorate the panelled hall of No. 4 with topographical views. A music book, opened at the beginning of an aria from an opera performed at the Haymarket in 1745, is painted above the door leading to the staircase. Heidegger died at his home in 1749, and is said to be buried in the churchyard.

The next occupant of the house was the extremely wealthy widow of Elias Levy. She was as kind and hospitable as she was eccentric, and frequently entertained royalty there. She died in 1805 at the age of 97. Her life story and those of her husband and other influential

Jews of Richmond and its neighbourhood are told in a small, privately printed book *Richmond and its Jewish Connections*, by Arthur Howitt, the first Jewish Mayor of Richmond, who held office from 1924 to 1925 and was re-elected Mayor in 1927. Nearer our own time the house was occupied by Charles Garvice, the romantic novelist who was extremely popular in the first two decades of the twentieth century, but is now almost forgotten. He died in 1920, and is buried in Richmond cemetery.

The present theatre, built in 1899, has been much abused by most writers on Richmond for its complete incongruity with the old houses around the Green, but is now on the GLC list of buildings scheduled as of architectural merit—chiefly on account of the Shakespearean characters in relief-work in the auditorium, and the gilded mouldings and plasterwork. It is a highly successful Repertory Theatre.

There were two previous theatres at Richmond. The first, in the early eighteenth century, was replaced by the Theatre Royal, which opened in 1766 with a prologue especially written by David Garrick. Edmund Kean leased it in 1831, but died in Richmond two years later. All the leading Georgian and Victorian actors appeared there before it closed in 1884.

Surrey's most famous delicacy, Maids of Honour cakes, were sold for over a century and a half at the original shop, No. 3 Hill Street, which was demolished recently. There are conflicting opinions on the date of origin of these delicious little cheesecakes. The *Oxford Dictionary* gives the date as 1769, which confirms the tradition that they were concocted for the occupants of Maids of Honour Row, but the *Country Life* recipe book published in 1932 gives a recipe said to have been taken from a cookery manuscript of Elizabeth I's reign, and some accounts connect them with Anne Boleyn, when Maid of Honour, and Henry VIII. Many versions of the recipe exist, but the secret of those made in the original shop was bought by Newens, whose cake shop in Kew Road carries on the long tradition.

St Mary Magdalene Church has a Perpendicular west tower of flint, but the remainder is a curious blending of Georgian and Victorian brickwork. The great interest lies in the many memorials in the church and churchyard. The earliest is a brass in memory of

Richard Cotton, an 'officer of the Wardroppe' to Mary Tudor and Elizabeth I.

There is a brass plate to James Thomson, the poet who lived and died at Richmond; a portrait medallion to Charles Kean, and another to Miss Braddon, sister of Sir Edward Braddon, Governor of Tasmania, wife of the publisher, James Maxwell, and mother of the novelist, W. B. Maxwell. The inscription describes her as 'a writer of rare and refined scholarship', which is rather higher praise than is given now, even to her best known novel, *Lady Audley's Secret.*

A kneeling figure in a niche over the south doorway commemorates Mary Anne Yates, the tragic actress, who was highly praised by Oliver Goldsmith and moved David Garrick to tears. Her husband, Richard Yates, is said to have been unequalled as a Shakespearean clown, but it would appear his temperament was more choleric than cheerful, as he died in a fit of rage because he could not have eels for his dinner!

On the outer wall of the church is a monument to Lord Fitzwilliam, founder of the Fitzwilliam Museum at Cambridge. Buried in the churchyard is Nicholas Brady, a royal chaplain and rector of Richmond from 1696 until his death in 1726. In collaboration with Nahum Tate he prepared the metrical version of the Psalms, which William of Orange ordered to be used in all churches.

Among notable people buried in Richmond cemetery are Sir Charles Hawtrey, the actor manager; Leslie Stuart, composer of *Soldiers of the Queen* and other popular Victorian songs; Arthur St John Adcock, the Fleet Street journalist and novelist who died in 1930, and two VCs, General Olperts of the Indian Mutiny, and Sergeant Harry Hampton of the South African War.

St Philip and All Saints Church, at the corner of Atwood Avenue and Marksbury Avenue, is known as the Barn Church. The plain exterior conceals a genuine sixteenth-century interior brought from Oxted. The barn was offered by the owners in 1926, when new churches were urgently needed in the diocese, and its fittings were brought from other churches far and near.

Probably the most frequently quoted descriptions of the view from Richmond Hill are those of Scott in *The Heart of Midlothian,* and Thomson, who describes it in 'Summer', in *The Seasons.* Richmond reluctantly admits that although there is a public house near the Richmond Park Gate called *The Lass of Richmond Hill*, the popular ballad of that name refers to Richmond Hill in Yorkshire.

There is a group of interesting and attractive houses on Richmond Hill. No. 3 The Terrace, attributed to Sir Robert Taylor, was built for Christopher Blanchard, George III's card-maker. It is said that when the king heard it was Blanchard's house, he exclaimed 'Why, all his cards must have turned up trumps'.

On the crest of the hill are The Wick, a perfect Georgian house designed by Robert Mylne in 1775, and Wick House, which was built by Sir Robert Chambers for Sir Joshua Reynolds in 1772. Sir Joshua used it at week-ends, and entertained Dr Johnson, Boswell, Edmund Burke and Oliver Goldsmith there. It was from a window in the drawing room that Sir Joshua painted one of his few landscapes—the enchanting view over the Thames.

The enormous Star and Garter Home, on the site of the fashionable Georgian Star and Garter Hotel, commands a magnificent view to solace the disabled servicemen who live there.

Richmond College, a beautiful building in Bath stone, was built in 1841–3 as a Wesleyan Theological Institution. The chapel has a pulpit brought from The Foundry, Moorfields, from which both John and Charles Wesley had preached on many occasions. Among the most distinguished students at the College were Dr Leslie Weatherhead, preacher, author and broadcaster, who was for many years minister of the City Temple; Hugh Price Hughes, a social reformer, and Editor of the *Methodist Times*, which he made into a powerful influence on Methodism; and Owen Spencer Watkins, who entered the College in 1893, became an Army Chaplain, and was the first Nonconformist to be appointed Honorary Chaplain to the King. He was later Deputy Chaplain General, and retired to become Administrative Padre to Toc H.

In its earliest years, Richmond College was one of the foremost centres for sending Methodist missionaries to the far corners of the earth. They were certainly well prepared for 'roughing it'! In *Richmond College 1843–1943*, A. J. Norman, who went there in 1883, recalls the stark routine. A monitor came round every morning at 6 a.m. to make sure every student was already at work. No one was allowed to leave the grounds after tea—not even to post a letter home. Travelling by train or bus on Sundays was not permitted, which meant that the student preachers walked as much as 15 miles to take a service in some remote suburban chapel. There was a special weekly fast-day on Fridays, sports were not encouraged and total abstinence was the rule.

In spite of this initial spartan training, many of the missionaries died of their hardships at an early age. Among them was Joseph Race, who entered the College in 1870, went to China as a missionary, and died there of typhoid at the age of 32. His brief but noble life has been the subject of a TV documentary by his grandson, Steve Race, the musician and broadcaster. During his years in China, Joseph Race learned to love the Chinese, and studied their traditions and culture. He built up a carefully chosen collection of coins which is now in the Gulbenkian Museum at Durham.

Richmond College is affiliated to the University of London.

Among many notable residents of Richmond was Sir William Temple, who married Dorothy Osborne in 1654 or 55, and settled at 'Sheen' in 1665–6. He planted an orangery and cultivated wall-fruit, which Evelyn thought 'the most exquisite nailed and trained, far better than ever I noted it'. Temple removed to Moor Park, near Farnham, in 1680. Although Esther Johnson ('Stella') was born in Richmond, and her widowed mother was in attendance on Sir William's widowed sister, the claim that Swift met 'Stella' at Richmond seems incorrect, as he did not enter Sir William's service until 1689.

George Hilditch spent most of his life in Richmond, and became known as 'The Richmond Painter'. He was the father of Alderman J. B. Hilditch, who was Mayor of Richmond in 1899. George's brother, Richard Hilditch, also lived at Richmond.

Mme de Staël lived for a while at Gothic House; the Royal Hospital in Kew Foot Road incorporates the house where James Thomson lived until his death; George Eliot and G. H. Lewes settled at 8 Park Street, in 1855, where she wrote *Scenes of Clerical Life* and *Adam Bede*.

Edward Jesse, the topographical writer, who was the last Deputy Surveyor to the Commissioners of Woods, Forests and Land Revenues, is believed to have died at his home in Sheen Lane. Leonard and Virginia Woolf lived from 1914 to 1924 at Suffield House, Paradise Road, where they set up the Hogarth Press and printed, among other works, the early poems of T. S. Eliot; and Richard Dimbleby, appointed the first News Observer to the BBC in 1936, was Chairman and Managing Director of the group of local papers acquired by his grandfather until his death in 1965.

Beautiful as the old buildings of Richmond are, the glory of the town is Richmond Park, which has been open freely to the public since the valiant John Lewis, a brewer of Richmond, brought an action against the gatekeeper, who had excluded him on the orders of Princess Amelia. He won a right of way for pedestrians at the Surrey Assizes at Kingston in 1758, but the Princess created more difficulties, and he brought another successful action against her. This public-spirited man fell into great poverty as a result of the expense of these lawsuits, and the flooding of his brewery, and it is to the credit of the Vicar, Thomas Wakefield, that he persuaded the people of Richmond to contribute towards a small annuity for their benefactor. Lewis died in 1792, and was buried in the churchyard. His tomb has since disappeared, but there is a portrait of him in Richmond Public Library.

The park covers about 2,358 acres, and is two and a half miles across from east to west and from north to south. It has all the charm of hills commanding far-reaching views, sheltered valleys, plantations, rhododendron thickets, old oak trees, open heaths and herds of red and fallow deer—so perfectly described by the Scottish poet, Patrick Chalmers, in his book of poems *Green Days and Blue Days*.

Only a road on the perimeter is open to motor traffic. The rest is for those who go on foot, and can appreciate the wonderful peace and seclusion of the park.

Richmond Park was enclosed in 1637 for Charles I. It was given to the City of London by Cromwell's Parliament, but prudently handed back to Charles II at the Restoration. A number of private residences are scattered unobtrusively in the park, each with interesting associations. Sheen Lodge was occupied from 1862 to 1892 by Sir Richard Owen, first Director of the Natural History Museum. He entertained Dickens, Millais and Gladstone at the Lodge.

Pembroke Lodge, where Lord John Russell, twice Prime Minister, lived, is now a restaurant and tea house. Thatched House Lodge is the home of HRH Princess Alexandra and her husband, the Hon. Angus Ogilvie, and White Lodge, built by George III, was the home of the Duke and Duchess of Teck, parents of Queen Mary. Their grandson, the Duke of Windsor, was born there in 1896. It is now the Royal Ballet School, and can be seen only by special appointment.

On the river bank below Richmond Hill are the Petersham Meadows. The small village of Petersham has an unusual number of aristocratic houses, among which are Montrose House, with its great iron gates, dating from the early eighteenth century; Petersham House, dating from the seventeenth century, with a staircase embellished with wall paintings by Louis Laguerre; and Rutland Lodge, of somewhat earlier date, which was damaged by fire in 1967, and has been converted into flats. Just off the drive to Ham House is the eighteenth-century Douglas House, home of the Duchess of Queensberry who was the patron of John Gay. Charles Dickens, who lived at Elm Lodge in 1839, wrote part of *Nicholas Nickleby* there. Sudbrook Park, between Petersham and Ham, is now a part of Richmond Park. The club house of the Sudbrook Park Golf Course was built in 1726 by James Gibbs for the second Duke of Argyll. Its main feature is an ornate double-cube room with decorations which show Gibbs at his most baroque.

The attractive church of St Peter, with its thirteenth-century chancel and later brickwork, has box pews, an eighteenth-century two-decker pulpit and a raised reading desk. There are seventeenth-century effigies of George Cole and his wife and grandson, and a monument in the south transept set up by the Hudson Bay Company in 1841 to the memory of Captain George Vancouver, who died in 1798. The Earl and Countess of Strathmore, parents of HM Queen Elizabeth the Queen Mother, were married in the church.

The seventeenth-century Ham House is the largest of its period in Surrey. Built by Sir Thomas Vavasour in 1610, it came into the possession of William Murray, 'whipping boy' to the Prince of Wales, afterwards Charles I, who created him Earl of Dysart. The house was enlarged and redecorated in the flamboyant style of the period by Dysart, and by his daughter, who succeeded him as Countess of Dysart in her own right, and married John Maitland, Duke of Lauderdale, as her second husband. It remained in the possession of their descendants until handed over to the National Trust in 1948. It is now administered by the Victoria and Albert Museum, which publishes an excellent illustrated guide to the house. Several inventories of the contents survive, and as far as possible the furniture has been replaced where it stood originally. Among the paintings is a portrait of the Duke and Duchess of Lauderdale which is considered to be the finest ever painted by Lely. There is a wonderful collection of seventeenth- and eighteenth-century costumes worn by the Dysart family, the interest of which is enhanced by the fact that some of the costumes are depicted in the family portraits. Ham House is open all the year round at advertised hours.

St Andrew's Church, on Ham Common, dates from 1830. It has a small brass in memory of Edward S. Borrodaile, who was lost in the Northern Territory of Australia with his companion Pearmain. A small red cross on the map of the Northern Territory engraved on the brass marks the place where they disappeared. Mount Borrodaile and Mount Pearmain in Australia are named in memory of their exploration. Sir Richard Owen is buried in the churchyard.

Although there has been considerable housing development at Ham, the original village nucleus of seventeenth- and eighteenth-century houses remains around Ham Common.

Kingston upon Thames is a busy commercial centre which takes pride in its history. The first recorded reference to Kingston is dated 838, when King Egbert held a Great Council there. The document, now in the British Museum, describes Kingston as 'that renowned place which is called Cyngestun in the region of Suthregia'.

The Coronation Stone outside the modern Guildhall is believed to mark the site of the Saxon palace, and to be the actual stone on which seven Saxon kings were crowned in the tenth century.

Among other survivals hidden away among a mass of modern buildings are three of the Conduit Houses and an inspection point built in connection with Cardinal Wolsey's conduit; Cleeve's Almshouses, founded in 1668; the Lovekyn Chapel of St Mary

Magdalene, founded in 1309, rebuilt in 1352, and much restored in 1886, which is now scheduled as an Ancient Monument; twelfth-century Clatterne Bridge, and much ancient woodwork hidden behind modern façades.

The parish church of All Saints has some thirteenth- and four-teenth-century details, but is virtually a Victorian building, and is of interest chiefly for its monuments, which include one of Chantrey's best works.

Kingston Museum has relics of the Anglo-Saxon and later period of the town's history, including pictures and maps. It also has a zooproxiscope—an early form of cinematograph—invented by Eadweard Muybridge, a native of the town. Muybridge went to the United States of America, where he became director of photographic studies to the US Government. He died at Kingston in 1904.

The Royal Borough of Kingston now includes Chessington, Coombe, Malden and Surbiton, and many well-known people have had associations with the area. Edward Gibbon, the historian of the Roman Empire, and R. C. Sherriff, the playwright, attended the Kingston Grammar School. General Eisenhower, Supreme Commander of Allied Forces in Europe, used Telegraph Cottage at Kingston Hill as a wartime residence during 1943 and 1944; George Meredith lived for a while in London Road, and John Galsworthy was brought up at Coombe, which he refers to as Robin Hill in *The Forsyte Saga*. Chessington Hall was the home of Fanny Burney's beloved 'Daddy Crisp', and the Chessington Zoo occupies the site of Burnt Stub, a fourteenth-century house burned down to a 'stub' by Parliamentarians during the Civil War.

Among those either commemorated in the parish church or buried in the borough are George Bate, the Court physician, who was one of the first elected Fellows of the Royal Society, and is especially remembered for his contribution towards the treatment of rickets; Thomas Hansard, jnr., editor of the *Parliamentary Debates*; A. C. Ranyard, a brilliant scientist who was Secretary of the Royal Astronomical Society, and Harry Hawker, the famous Australian-born airman.

When Kingston was taken over by London in 1965, it created the anomaly that Surrey's County Council Offices were outside the county. Plans are now being made to build new County Council Offices at Guildford, and to transfer the administrative headquarters there when completed. At the time of writing (October 1974), I have been informed by Mr Keith Bassett, the Public Relations and Information Officer at the present County Council Offices in Kingston, that the basic design for the new County Hall has been chosen, and it is hoped to make use of a site in Stoke Park, north of the A3 Guildford by-pass.

There are many advantages attaching to this site, but as a planning enquiry must be held, planning permission obtained from the Secretary of State for the Environment, and a Bill promoted in Parliament, before work can begin, it is likely to be some years before the new County Hall is completed. If the Stoke Park site is not approved, it could take even longer.

Surbiton has memories of Richard Jefferies, the naturalist, and Thomas Hardy, who began his married life there. Surbiton's tree-shaded promenade looks across the Thames to the park and gardens of Hampton Court Palace, and its suburban streets spread out to Long Ditton and the boundary of present-day Surrey.

CHAPTER THREE

The Thames Valley

The Dittons to Egham, and Staines to Sunbury

The Thames has long been the playground of boating enthusiasts, anglers and ornithologists. In recent years, sailing clubs, boat yards, marinas and reservoirs have proliferated to an unprecedented extent, and even the most ardent lover of Surrey must admit there have been some disastrously badly planned developments between the River Thames and the North Downs. Nevertheless, there are still long reaches of the river bordered by meadows and trees, and not all modern building has been bad.

The Dittons, the Moleseys, Walton and Weybridge follow each other in quick succession. There are the remains of a genuine riverside village at Thames Ditton, with weather-boarded houses, and a gem of an anglers' inn, The Swan, and at Weston Green old houses cluster round the village green and pond in true Surrey style. Imber Court, once a seat of the Onslow family, is now a training establishment of the Metropolitan Police.

The River Mole, from which the Moleseys derive their name, flows into the Thames just below the bridge which carries the A309 across the Thames to Hampton Court Palace.

Hurst Park Race Course has disappeared under a new housing estate, and great reservoirs rise high above the rows of houses, but there are attractive old buildings and interesting modern architectural experiments scattered among the more monotonous streets. The unpromising exterior of the Victorian church of East Molesey has brasses from the earlier church, including one to 'Antonie Stonden, cupbearer to the King of Scotland, some tyme Lord Darnley, father to King James of England'. All Saints Church, West Molesey,

48

has a Perpendicular tower and font, and a Jacobean pulpit with its sounding board.

It is at Walton and Weybridge that the genius of Surrey for salvaging beautiful open spaces from encroaching developments begins to manifest itself. Walton-on-Thames, so called to distinguish it from Walton-on-the-Hill, is first mentioned in Domesday Book, but many prehistoric finds have been made there, some of which can be seen in the Weybridge Museum. The tradition persists that Cowey Stakes, near Walton Bridge, is the place where Caesar and his army crossed the Thames to attack Cassivelaunus, although the exact location of the crossing has been disputed.

The fifteenth-century half-timbered manor-house was once the home of John Bradshaw, who presided over the judges who condemned Charles I to death. He is said to haunt the house. Admiral Rodney was born in 1717 at No. 17 Church Street; 47 High Street* was the home of General Ireton, who married Oliver Cromwell's daughter, Bridget, and Sir Arthur Sullivan lived at River House, Manor Road, now owned by the Council.

It was at Walton that Cecil Hepworth had his film studio. He was a major force in the silent film industry in Britain in its earliest days, and invented a Vivaphone in an attempt to synchronize the mouthings of the screen actors to a gramophone record—not always successfully!

St Mary's Church dates in part from the Norman period, and has some interesting monuments. William Lilly, the astrologer, is buried in the church, and is commemorated by a 'faire black marble stone' placed there by his friend Elias Ashmole, founder of the Ashmolean Museum at Oxford. Lilly predicted the Great Fire of London, and when it broke out, was accused of having caused it, but managed to prove his innocence.

The sixteenth-century Selwyn brasses commemorate John Selwyn, Keeper of Oatlands Park, and his family. Selwyn is shown riding on the back of a stag, and plunging his knife into its throat, picturing his exploit in guiding a stag towards Elizabeth I, and stabbing it dead at her feet.

There is also an enormous monument by Roubiliac to Field-Marshal Richard Boyle, Viscount Shannon.

* Demolished 1974.

Outstanding among some fine examples of modern architecture at Walton is the Town Hall, with its graceful curve, completed in 1966.

Three miles south, at Burhill, is Whiteley Village, built by William Whiteley, 'The Universal Provider', whose splendid emporium in Queen's Road, Bayswater, was too dignified to be called a 'shop'! When Whiteley died in 1907, he left a million pounds to build a village to which old people could retire. Houses designed by the foremost architects of the day, and all the amenities of a village, including churches, library, a post office and recreational facilities were attractively laid out among trees, lawns and flower beds, on a 225-acre site, and still form an ideal place for retirement.

Not far from Whiteley Village is the King's House, given by Royal Warrant holders to mark the Silver Jubilee of George v, to enable the King to nominate some especially honoured servant of the Crown to live there. It was fitted with every device then known to science, and everything was British, home-made and home-grown, or sent by the Dominions overseas. Its first tenant was Admiral Sir Reginald Tupper, who commanded the fleet of armed merchantmen and trawlers patrolling the sea between Scotland and Iceland in the Second World War. It is now a private house called Kingsmere.

Weybridge's history is chiefly bound up with that of the royal palace at Oatlands, the park of which extended over into Walton. Originally a small farm, it was purchased about 1476 by Sir Bartholomew Rede, a former Lord Mayor of London, who built a large house there. This was acquired in 1537 by Henry viii, who built the palace on a site nearer the river, for his fourth Queen, Anne of Cleves. Charles i's fourth son, Henry of Oatlands and Duke of Gloucester, was born there, and it remained a royal residence until demolished by the Parliamentarians in 1650. The masonry was used by Sir Richard Weston, of Sutton Place, to construct the Wey Navigation Canal.

After the Restoration, Sir Bartholomew Rede's house was rebuilt several times. When Frederica, Duchess of York, separated from her husband (one of Queen Victoria's 'wicked uncles') she retired to Oatlands, but they remained on amicable terms. He frequently entertained his friends there, while the Duchess devoted herself to the care of her pets. Following the death of the Duke of York in 1827, it was purchased by Edward Hughes Ball, nicknamed 'Golden Ball', said to have been the richest man in England. He reconstructed it. In 1856 it was converted into the Oatlands Park Hotel.

The monument erected by the people of Weybridge to the memory of the eccentric but much loved Duchess originally stood in Seven Dials, St Giles's Circus, London. It was designed by Edward Pierce, the seventeenth-century sculptor, and is the only example of his work in Surrey.

Brooklands House was built by Lord King in 1822, and the famous Brooklands motor-race course was built by his grandson, Hugh Locke-King, in 1907. The first flying meeting was held in October 1909. The motor racing circuit was abandoned before the 1939–45 war, but it is said that the roar of engines and the scream of tyres can be heard still at times, and that the ghost of Percy Lambert, the racing motorist who was killed on the track in 1913, haunts the British Aircraft Corporation factory built over part of the course.

Eastlands, in Brooklands Lane, was once the home of Fanny Kemble, who describes it in her *Recollections of a Girlhood*. More recently it was the home of Warwick Deeping, author of *Forest Lovers, Richard Yea-and-Nay* and other popular novels, until his death in 1950.

The Victorian church has some very good brasses, and a Chantrey memorial to Frederica, Duchess of York.

Attached to the Roman Catholic church of St Charles Borromeo is a small domed and castellated mausoleum where the exiled King Louis Philippe was buried in 1850.

Trees and open fields overlook this reach of the river, where the Desborough Cut by-passes Halliford, on the north bank. The Cut was opened by Lord Desborough of Taplow Court, a remarkable athlete, who was a punting champion for many years, and in 1835 was stroke of a racing eight which crossed the English Channel. The Cut rejoins the main stream at D'Oyly Carte Island, just below Shepperton Lock, where the Wey Navigation flows into the Thames.

Between Shepperton Lock and Chertsey Lock, the river makes a leisurely curve round the Chertsey Meads. Chertsey was a very small place when I first knew it, but since the 1939–45 war it has been growing steadily, and is now facing upheaval with a grandiose scheme for the re-development of the town centre, and the proximity of two new motorways, the M3 and M25.

Chertsey Abbey virtually disappeared at the Dissolution, when its stones were carted away for building Hampton Court Palace. Excavations carried out in the nineteenth century yielded many encaustic tiles and some coffins, now dispersed in various museums.

The Abbey was founded in the seventh century by Frithwald of Surrey, who gave the land, and St Erkenwald of Lincolnshire, the first Abbot, who was afterwards Bishop of London. In the early centuries of its existence, it had a very chequered history, but Abbot Wulfhold was one of the few Saxon abbots not displaced at the Conquest, and the abbey rose to immense riches, power and possessions before its dissolution.

There is hardly anything to be seen on the site, which is skirted by the Abbey River, but one of its six bells survives in the parish church. It rings the curfew from Michaelmas to Lady Day, and is said to have tolled for Henry VI when his body was brought secretly to Chertsey after his murder in the Tower of London.

The bell is also associated with the legend of Blanche Heriot, whose sweetheart was imprisoned at Chertsey during the Wars of the Roses. He was condemned to die at the ringing of the curfew, and his pardon was delayed, so Blanche heroically clung to the clapper of the bell to prevent it sounding until her lover was reprieved. Most schoolchildren of my generation knew by heart *Curfew Must not Ring To-night*, but few seem to learn it now. The poem was written by the American poetess, Rosa Hartwick Thorpe, when she was a schoolgirl, and published in 1870. She altered Blanche's name to Bessie, and transferred the action to the struggle between Royalists and Parliamentarians, but she captured the imagination of the English-speaking world.

Albert Smith, who was born in Chertsey, and joined his doctor father in practice there for a few years, wrote a play, *Blanche Heriot*, which gave the legend more correctly. It was produced at the Surrey Theatre in 1849, but did not have such a resounding success as the poem. Smith is remembered today only as one of the original contributors to *Punch*, and for his vivid *Sketches of London Life and Character*.

7 (opposite) *View of Box Hill from Ranmore Common*

The site of Porch House, where Abraham Cowley lived, and dedicated his essay on *The Garden* to John Evelyn, is now covered with shops. The panelling is in America.

St Peter's Church is largely rebuilt, but has a medieval chapel, some fifteenth-century work, and several monuments, including one by Westmacott, and one dated 1819 by Flaxman. There is also a memorial to Cowley, whose wife is buried in the churchyard, and a tablet to Charles James Fox the Whig statesman, who spent the last years of his life in a house on St Anne's Hill. Although only a little over 250 feet in height, the hill stands out in the surrounding low-lying country, and is a well-known viewpoint from which, it is said, St Paul's Cathedral can be seen on a clear day.

Beyond Chertsey, the Thames winds well north to Egham, which can be reached by the A320 skirting Thorpe on the east, or the B388, which runs through the centre of the village.

Thorpe is the only place in Surrey within easy reach of the Thames which remains indisputably a village, although how long it can remain so is problematical, with the proximity of the M3 and M25, which cross on the south-west, and a million-pound Water Park being built in disused gravel pits to the south.

Few of the motorists who rush between Chertsey and Egham suspect the existence of the village, and even those who motor through it seldom notice anything but the Red Lion. This inn is first mentioned in 1700, and is probably older. It faces Coldharbour Lane, which turns off between forbiddingly high walls, behind which are Thorpe Place, a gracious brick house built in 1801, and Spelthorne St Mary, a late eighteenth-century house with some fine gates brought from Feltham, Middlesex, and a seventeenth-century barn. It now belongs to an Anglican community.

Beyond Spelthorne St Mary is a tiny village square, dominated by St Mary's Church, which has a low, seventeenth-century brick tower. Although much restored, it dates from the twelfth century, and has fine brasses to the Bonde and Denham families, including some palimpsests, and interesting monuments, details of which are given in the guide to the church. An unusual feature is an ancient brass Russian ikon.

Farther east along Coldharbour Lane is Eastley End. In June

1972, I visited the beautifully restored Georgian mansion, which had just been opened, with a flourish of publicity, as an exclusive restaurant—yet less than a year later it had become the offices of the Water Park.

Frederick Turner's *History of Thorpe* says the original owners of the manor were the de Thorpes, who were first mentioned in 1189. The name of the family continues to crop up until the fifteenth century, but the de Graveneys appear to have got possession of the manor in 1217, and held it until 1337. Both the lords of the manor and their tenants were in frequent dispute with the Abbots of Chertsey, and in 1369, the men of Thorpe joined with those of Egham and Chobham to attack the monastery, and burned the Court Rolls. Thorpe men also joined in the Peasant's Revolt of 1381, but their subsequent history seems to have been less militant.

The North Country landscape painter, Henry Dawson, who had been living in Croydon, where he was encouraged by Ruskin, bought a small house at Thorpe in 1853, and painted a number of local scenes, including *Hay Time on Thorpe Green*, *The Bells of Ouseley* and *Runnymede*. He moved to Chiswick in 1859.

Another artist, Berkshire-born William Henry Knight, who specialized in scenes of everyday life, rented Thorpe Vicarage for a while.

It is believed the Roman road to Silchester crossed the north of the parish at Thorpe Lea. A large brass of Trajan, and a small brass of Carausius, were found nearby.

Several of the beautiful old houses in the neighbourhood have been demolished, or so altered they are unrecognizable, but happily Great Fosters survives. Brayley thought the house took its name from the Foster family, but it is mentioned as 'Fforsters' in the will of Sir John Dodderidge, Solictor-General to James I, who died at Great Fosters in 1628, and Sir Robert Foster, who became Lord Chief Justice at the Restoration, did not live at Great Fosters before 1630. He died in 1663, and is buried in Egham church. The name may be a corruption of foresters, when it was a hunting lodge in Windsor Forest, which then covered the whole area.

The date over the porch at Great Fosters is 1598, and the fabric is chiefly Elizabethan, incorporating earlier work. It is the magnificent interior which is so memorable, with its splendid Jacobean woodwork, richly decorated plaster ceilings and carved stone mantelpieces. The formal garden at the rear of the house is surrounded on three sides by a moat, beyond which is a rose-garden and lawns. It is now an hotel.

Egham, on the southern bank, and Staines, which comes down to the water's edge on the north, are linked by road and rail bridges, but remain very distinctly apart. Egham's newer houses are springing up chiefly on the south, but reach the river at The Hythe.

Egham's railway station, most unusually, is so close to its shopping centre that it is a matter for congratulation that the curving High Street, although it has no outstanding building, still has all the air of a small country town—largely because, so far, the newer shops are not tower blocks, out of all proportion to the older buildings, and the A30 by-passes Egham on the north.

The number of Egham's inns testifies to its former importance as a coaching centre, but most of them have been completely rebuilt, although parts of the Red Lion date from the seventeenth century. Strode School, founded in 1704, was rebuilt in 1915, but with its well-kept lawns it has a mellow, old-world look.

The Egham Literary and Scientific Institute, which took its present form in 1846, maintains a museum which is open to the public on Saturdays.

Much of Egham belonged to Chertsey Abbey, and passed to the Crown at its dissolution. The most distinguished of the landowners was Sir John Denham, who was appointed Lord Chief Baron of the Irish Exchequer in 1609, and Baron of the English Exchequer in 1617, in which office he earned the encomium of Bacon as a 'prudent and politic administrator'. He died in 1630, and was succeeded by his son, also Sir John, Surveyor and Solicitor-General, who took up residence at Egham after his first marriage. His well-known poem *Cooper's Hill*, describing the scenery around his Egham home, was first published in 1642.

The entrance to Egham churchyard is still approached through a fifteenth-century lich-gate, but the old church of St John the Baptist was rebuilt in 1817, in a style variously described as one of 'simple and severe beauty', 'very ugly', and 'an interesting specimen of early nineteenth century architecture'. It is notable for the oval cupola surmounting the tower, and however much opinions may differ on the architecture, there can be no disagreement about the unusual interest of its memorials. The oldest tablet records that Abbot Rutherwyke of Chertsey Abbey rebuilt the chancel of the church in 1327. The extraordinary Denham monuments are in the vestibules. Sir John Denham, the elder, is shown rising from the grave in a winding sheet, above a charnel house of skeletons, and his two wives appear in startlingly naturalistic painted reliefs.

The hymn-writer, J. S. B. Monsell, was vicar of Egham before becoming rector of St Nicholas, Guildford, where he died in 1875 from injuries received in a fall from the roof of his church when it was undergoing repairs.

West of the Runnymede roundabout the A308 follows the river bank across the historic fields of Runnymede. It is an established fact that the barons gathered on the Meads in 1215, but it is less certain whether King John set his seal to Magna Charta there, or on Magna Charta Island, which is privately owned. The whole of the Meads, with two memorial buildings and two kiosks designed by Sir Edwin Lutyens, guarding the east and west entrance, are owned by the National Trust. Part of the wooded slopes of Cooper's Hill, which border the Meads on the south, was given to the Trust by Egham Council in 1963.

As if the significance of Magna Charta were not enough to make Runnymede hallowed ground, the sublimely simple and inexpressibly moving Commonwealth Air Force Cloister Memorial, designed by Sir Edward Maufe, was opened by HM The Queen in 1953. Set on Cooper's Hill, it commands a view of the Meads and the winding river, and far north over the chequered fields beyond, which seems unchanged since Sir John Denham wrote his poem, for modern developments are hidden by trees or softened by distance.

The memorial commemorates the 20,455 airmen from all parts of the British Commonwealth and Empire who died during the Second World War in the cause of the freedom established by Magna Charta.

On the slopes below, and closer to the river, is the Magna Charta Memorial set up by the American Bar Association in 1957, and the

Kennedy Memorial in an acre of woodland given by the Crown. It was built by public subscription, in memory of President John F. Kennedy, and was unveiled by HM The Queen in 1965.

At the western end of Runnymede is the hostelry, the Bells of Ouseley, just over the Berkshire border, and Priest's Hill road (A238) climbing up to Englefield Green.

Englefield Green has altered very little around the large green itself, although many new houses have sprung up, particularly along Egham Hill, which is dominated by the enormous bulk of Holloway College. Thomas Holloway, who made a fortune with his patent medicines, built and endowed a Ladies' College in memory of his devoted wife, who died in 1875. He bought 93 acres of land, and commissioned W. H. Crosland to build a college on the model of the Château of Chambord, in an overwhelming riot of red-brick towers and cupolas, picked out in white. There were a thousand rooms for the 250 students, and a magnificent Picture Gallery. It was opened by Queen Victoria in 1886, and remained a ladies' college until 1965, when men students were admitted for the first time. It is now a constituent college of the University of London.

The Picture Gallery, which contains works by British artists of the eighteenth and nineteenth centuries, including Constable, Gainsborough, Turner, Crome, Millais, Landseer, Morland, Frith and Fildes, is open free on certain days.

Thomas Holloway also, on the advice of Lord Shaftesbury, built at Virginia Water, a much-needed sanatorium for the mentally sick, which was opened in 1885.

Many 'elegant villas' sprang up on 'Ingfield Heath'—the former name of Englefield Green—in the eighteenth century, and several celebrities have lived there. Shelley made a brief stay in 1845, and wrote *Alastor*. He also made friends with Dr Furnivall, a young physician who had a prosperous practice in Egham, and maintained a private lunatic asylum at his house, Great Fosters, from which he made a fortune. He attended Mary Shelley on the birth of her son at Marlow in 1817.

Dr Furnivall's son, Frederick James Furnivall, who was born at Egham, was a member of the Philological Society and editor of its *English Dictionary*, which developed into the *Oxford English Dictionary*.

His disinterested enthusiasm in organizing many societies for the purpose of printing manuscripts and editing English literature stimulated the development of English study at home and abroad, and he spared no pains to achieve completeness and accuracy. He was also a strong supporter of the Christian Socialist Movement.

Sir George Chesney, who is buried at Englefield Green, was the first Principal of the Royal Civil Engineering College on Cooper's Hill, which opened in 1871. He had suggested the establishment of the College, chosen the site, selected the staff and organized its courses. In the same year the College opened, he contributed a skit to Blackwood's Magazine called *The Battle of Dorking, or Reminiscences of a Volunteer*. This was an imaginary account of a successful invasion of England, intended to urge the development of the volunteer movement for national defence. It had a widespread popularity.

South-west of Englefield Green are Savill Garden and the Valley Gardens, almost all of which are in Surrey, although Windsor Great Park, of which they are a part, is over the Berkshire boundary.

The Savill Garden, which covers some 35 acres of woodland, was completed in 1939. It was named after Sir Eric Savill, then Deputy Ranger, who created this superb garden. Even the colour pictures in the lavishly illustrated guide are insufficient to show adequately the variety and beauty of the layout, the blending of colours and the alternation of herbaceous borders, rose gardens, woodland glades, ponds and alpine meadows, which ensure colour and interest from March to October, when the garden is open to the public.

The Valley Gardens, bordering the northern bank of Virginia Water, are open freely all the year round. Sir Eric Savill, with the encouragement of George vi, began the landscaping of the Valley Gardens in 1947. They cover 500 acres, and are especially noted for the wonderful range of flowering trees and shrubs, rhododendrons, azaleas, magnolias and camellias, which are in bloom from April to December. Sequoias, maples, red oaks and other rare trees are a blaze of red and gold in the autumn. There is also an extensive heather garden.

The peaceful beauty of the lake of Virginia Water owes its existence to William, Duke of Cumberland, then Ranger of Windsor Great Park. The actual planning was carried out by Thomas Sandby the draughtsman and architect, who had been appointed Deputy Ranger in 1746. He was assisted by his younger brother, Paul, the water-colour painter, who was a pioneer of topographical art in England. Today the vast expanse of water, with its many bays and promontories, and its woods and meadows, looks completely natural, and is frequented by many varieties of wildfowl.

Virginia Water is also the happy haunt of many day trippers in the summer, especially at week-ends, but they mostly stay in the area near the Wheatsheaf Hotel beside the London Road (A30), and it is easy to escape to perfect solitude, for the greater part remains as peaceful as it is in the depths of winter.

The Wentworth Golf Club, with its three courses, on which championship matches are played frequently, has attracted many wealthy residents to the Wentworth Estate at Virginia Water, south of the lake. Their houses and gardens have been sited with great care to preserve the natural pinewood landscape.

The area of Middlesex north of the Thames between Staines and Sunbury, which is now administratively in Surrey, has not yet been assimilated into Surrey life, which is not altogether surprising. The historic boundary of the Thames is still a barrier, in spite of the now numerous bridges, and the whole aspect of the area is utterly different. Its almost uniformly level acres have suffered not only from the impact of Londoners needing housing, but also from their ever-growing need for drinking-water. It is also cut up by motorways.

The lonely lanes edged by hedgerows of blackthorn, dog-roses, honeysuckle and blackberries, down which I cycled when a schoolgirl, and the meadows spangled with wild flowers, have disappeared under vast reservoirs with grassy banks so high it is impossible to see the water from road level. They dwarf the surrounding houses and hide the once entrancing view across the Thames to the Surrey hills. More recently, marinas have come into being, and disused gravel pits are filled with water. Motorways and housing estates take up almost all the land that is left.

It must be said, however, that the reservoirs have their own special attraction. As early as 1934, Sir William Beach Thomas, in *Yeoman's England*, was writing that the biggest flocks of duck he had seen anywhere were to be found on the Staines Reservoir, the great-crested grebe was quite common, and heron were breeding there. Today the number and variety of waterfowl have grown as the reservoirs have multiplied until the area now appears to have far more water than land. The villages have been almost engulfed, and much that should have been preserved has been swept away, or modernized out of all recognition, but a few links with a far-distant past remain.

The London Stone, in the little riverside park on the west of Staines, close to the Buckinghamshire boundary, marks the western limit of the jurisdiction of the City of London over the river, before the Thames Conservancy was formed in 1857.

Staines was the Roman *Ad Pontes*, where the great highway from London to Silchester and Bath crossed the Thames, and there has been a succession of bridges there through the centuries.

The parish church of St Mary is on a site traditionally associated with druidical worship, but was rebuilt in 1828 with the exception of the tower, which was once claimed to be the work of Inigo Jones. It is now acknowledged there is no evidence for this. A modern stained-glass window commemorates the consecration, in an earlier church on the site, of the Bishops of Bangor and St David's by Archbishop Stephen Langton, after the signing of Magna Charta.

The nineteenth-century Town Hall is the successor of the Market House where, owing to a plague in London, Sir Walter Raleigh was committed for trial for treason in 1603, but the Market Square is under threat of a redevelopment of quite horrifying hideousness.

Some of the old coaching inns remain, but such older buildings as have survived are to be found in or near Church Street, Binbury Row and Vicarage Road.

North of Staines the old hamlet of Yeoveney, and part of the manor of Poyle, which was owned in the time of Elizabeth I by Nicholas Hilliard, the greatest of all English miniature painters, have disappeared under the waters of the Wraysbury Reservoir.

The bridge over the little River Colne which runs through the centre of Colnbrook marks the dividing line between Buckinghamshire and Surrey. Close by, on the Surrey side, is the so-called 'King John's Palace', a picturesque half-timbered house dating from three or four centuries after his reign. It is yet another place which is the centre of a struggle for its survival.

Richard Cox, a retired brewer of Bermondsey, raised the first Cox's Orange Pippin at Lawn Cottage, Colnbrook, in the early nineteenth century. It was first advertised by the famous Slough firm of Charles Turner in 1850.

Stanwell Moor, split by the A3044, and largely covered by the King George VI and Staines Reservoirs, still has a large mill on the Horton Road. It is now a factory. The once small, quiet village of Stanwell is unrecognizable in its modern guise, apart from the seventeenth-century Lord Knyvett's School, now used as a community centre. It has been scheduled as an Ancient Monument. The kneeling effigies of Lord Knyvett and his wife Elizabeth were cut by Nicholas Stone in 1622, at a cost of £215. Stanwell parish church also has a brass of 1408 to Nicholas Thorp, a former rector, and a memorial to Thomas Windsor, the original lord of the manor. Stanwell Place, one of the finest Georgian houses in the district, was wantonly demolished within the last year or two, to make way for a gravel pit.

Rose growers should hold Stanwell in particular affection, for it was here that the *Rosa Spinosissima* shrub, Stanwell Perpetual, was discovered in 1838. Unlike most roses, which have a brief period of popularity and are then forgotten, it is still in the catalogues of the leading commercial rose growers today. It is also one of those recommended by the Royal National Rose Society, and its fragrant little blooms, varying from white to blush pink, are ideal for floral arrangements.

Ashford is now joined up with Staines on the east, between the Staines and Queen Mary Reservoirs. It is chiefly notable for the Welsh Girls' School, which was founded in Clerkenwell in 1718 by the Honourable and Loyal Society of Ancient Britons, a group of London Welshmen, to provide for the education and apprenticeship of Welsh children in London. The school moved to Ashford in 1857, and in 1881 became a Foundation School for the higher education of girls of Welsh parentage, whether born in London or elsewhere. The school had an extensive library of Welsh books and manuscripts, some of which were given to the British Museum in 1843, and the remainder are in the National Library of Wales at Aberystwyth.

The school was recognized by the Board of Education as a secondary school in 1918.

Charlton, as late as 1951, was so remote that it had no public transport, shops or electricity, but since then it has acquired these, and all too much more. Its chief feature now is the enormous filter beds of the Metropolitan Water Board, and it is close to the high bank of the Queen Mary Reservoir. The once fascinating Harrow Inn, reputed to be the oldest inhabited house in Middlesex, has been so tidied up that it no longer looks old.

Littleton, close to the southern bank of the same reservoir, is another remote village of Saxon origin which has been overtaken by modernity. The manor was bought in the eighteenth century by the Woods, of whom General Sir David Wood was the most distinguished. He fought in South Africa, the Crimea and in the Indian Mutiny, died in 1894, and was buried in the attractive little church of St Mary Magdalene, in the brick mausoleum built for the Woods in 1765. The church has work of various periods since the twelfth century, some very good fittings of carved woodwork, and a brass to Blanche Vaughan, dated 1553.

Sir John Millais frequently stayed at the seventeenth-century rectory, and after his death his widow gave the church a stained glass window reproducing one of his paintings.

Littleton Park, in which the Woods lived until it was partially burned down in 1874, is in the grounds of the Shepperton Studios, where such well-known British films as *Oliver!*, *Colditz*, *Richard III* and *The Guns of Navarone* have been produced. The studios were reorganized on a smaller scale in 1974.

Between Staines and Laleham is Penton Hook Lock, which by-passes the curious horseshoe bend of the main stream, with its tangle of wild flowers on the banks.

Laleham, if it cannot still boast the 'great charm' of 'entire loneliness' so much appreciated by Dr Arnold, has remained a little off the beaten track, with a rural appearance enhanced by the beautiful park bordering the river. It was formerly part of the Laleham Park estate bought by the Middlesex County Council as a public open space. Laleham House, with its handsome portico, was built in 1803 for the second Earl of Lucan, whose son was in command of the cavalry at Balaclava when his brother-in-law, Lord Cardigan, led the Charge of the Light Brigade. The house is now a nunnery.

Thomas Arnold and his family lived at Laleham for nine years before he became headmaster of Rugby, and his son, Matthew Arnold, the poet, returned to spend six years as the pupil of his parson uncle, James Buckland. Arnold's home was demolished in 1864, and its bricks were used to build a National School.

The nave arcades of All Saints' Church date from the late twelfth century, the massive tower from 1732, and the Lucan Chapel was added in the sixteenth century.

Shepperton, where the Thames makes a deep curve between Staines and Hampton Court, was formerly the most southerly parish in Middlesex. Shepperton's little central square has two old inns, the Anchor, with a carved oak porch, and the King's Head, with a modern sign showing the head of Charles II, to perpetuate the legend that he stayed there with Nell Gwyn.

The grouping of the buildings in the square, with the church and rectory, is still delightful, in spite of some unfortunate modern additions.

St Nicholas's Church is a picturesque jumble of periods, and has a gallery displaying the Hanoverian arms. Two of the handsome eighteenth-century gravestones in the churchyard bear Latin inscriptions to Benjamin and Cotto Blake, Negro servants, who both died in 1781. Thomas Love Peacock and several of his family, including his three-year-old daughter Margaret, for whom he composed a touching epitaph, are buried at Shepperton.

The fine old rectory was originally built in the fifteenth century, but has been enlarged. William Grocyn, who was rector from 1504 to 1513, was a friend of Erasmus, who is said to have visited him there. J. M. Neale also had associations with the rectory. He was a leader of the High Church movement, and the author or translator of many *Hymns Ancient and Modern*, including *Good King Wenceslaus*, *Jerusalem the Golden* and *O Happy Band of Pilgrims*. He is reputed to have spoken 24 languages. The rectory has other interesting associations, but contrary to a general belief, the Shepperton of George Eliot's *Scenes of Clerical Life* was not this village, but Chilvers Coton in her native Warwickshire.

Adjoining the church is the manor-house, built about 1830. Part of the lawn sloping down to the river is now a public park, and nearby is the Silent Pool, a pretty backwater.

There are a number of old houses in the neighbourhood of the square, some of which are built of the distinctive brown bricks formerly manufactured at Shepperton. The Magpie Hotel, in Thames Street, has a tablet recording that the first meeting of The Grand Order of Water Rats—the social and charitable organization of Variety Artists—was held there in 1889.

Shepperton Green and the Shepperton Film Studios, already mentioned, now lie north of the M3.

Shepperton and Lower Halliford owe much of their attraction to the Desborough Cut, which leaves the meandering main stream of the Thames comparatively free of boating traffic.

Thomas Love Peacock lived at Elmbank, Lower Halliford, for many years before his death in 1866. Here, he planted a weeping willow sent to him from St Helena by Sir Hudson Lowe, who was Governor during Napoleon's exile there. One of Peacock's daughters was the first wife of George Meredith, and their son, Arthur, was born at Elmbank.

About half a mile down the river, near Walton Bridge, is Cowey Stakes, mentioned in connection with Walton. Early Saxon cemeteries have been found nearby.

Beyond Walton Bridge there are innumerable bungalows with flower-filled gardens, blocks of flats and a succession of small islands.

Lower Sunbury clusters round St Mary's Church, near the river. St Mary's has an eighteenth-century tower surmounted by a cupola, and the interior was reconstructed in 1856 in the Byzantine style. It has galleries supported on cast-iron columns and heavily ornamented with mosaics, and a stone pulpit with a brilliant inlay. One commentator unkindly said the church was 'happily too dark [for it] to be easily seen'. The church was re-dedicated in 1972 after a much-needed restoration.

Oliver Twist and Bill Sikes are said to have slept under the churchyard yew before the Shepperton robbery in Dickens's *Oliver Twist*.

Bronze-Age burial sites were discovered on Sunbury Common in 1870. The Sunbury Charter, dated AD 962, in the muniment room of

Westminster Abbey, records the grant of 'Sunnabyri' to the Abbey, and gives a detailed list of landmarks, some of which can still be identified.

There are some attractive old houses in Sunbury, and a Victorian inn, The Flower Pot, with a Doric porch and a sign depicting the Virgin with a lily in a flower pot beside her. Sunbury Court, now a Salvation Army Youth Centre, dates from about 1770, and has wall paintings by Elias Martin, the Swedish painter who lived in England from 1768 to 1780. Unfortunately, the eighteenth-century Hawke House, home of Admiral 'Sea Hawke', and now owned by a property developer, has been badly damaged, first by vandals, and then by a demolition gang, in spite of the fact that it was a 'listed' building. The Residents' Association and Spelthorne Council are making great efforts to save it from further destruction.

The new Surrey boundary takes in Kempton Park Race Course, which is on the site of a palace of Eleanor of Provence, wife of Henry III. It fell into disrepair after 1680, and a new house was built for Sir Thomas Grantham in 1697, outside the boundary of the present race-course. Kempton Park has its own railway station, and has been modernized recently. The new Silver Ring Stand is claimed to be the finest in the country.

Gilbert White spent several summers at Sunbury, with his friend, the Rev. John Mulso, and in a letter to Thomas Pennant, dated 4 November 1767, recalls being 'much amused with those myriads of the swallow kind which assemble in those parts', and which, before migrating, 'roosted every night in the osier beds of that river instead of on chimneys and houses'.

CHAPTER FOUR

The Portsmouth Road

A glance at the map of Surrey will show that the old Portsmouth coach road (approximately the A3 of today) traverses the present county from Esher in the north-east to Hindhead and the Hampshire border in the south-west.

Esher, built on rising ground above the River Mole, has the site of an Iron-Age settlement nearby, and although the origin of the name has been disputed, it is generally agreed it was Saxon. It is mentioned in Domesday Book. It must always have been lively with traffic, which has brought an ever-increasing rise in size and population, and the consequent disappearance of many links with the past, but Esher is still worth more than a passing glance.

The Bear Inn, on the south side of the High Street, has been rebuilt, but preserves the gigantic jackboots of the postillion who rode one of the horses of the coach which brought Louis Philippe of France to exile at nearby Claremont, in 1848. The Bear has been identified with 'The Bull' where Sherlock Holmes and Watson found 'comfortable quarters' when investigating *The Adventure of Wisteria Lodge*.

Hiding behind the Bear Inn is the former parish church which, after years of neglect, is now being well cared for. It dates from about 1540. The brick south chapel, added in 1725 as the family pew of the Duke of Newcastle, who was then living at Claremont, and his brother, Henry Pelham, who was living at Esher Place, was divided into two separate rooms, each with its own fireplace. The pew has handsome Corinthian columns facing towards the chancel, and can only be entered from outside the church. Among the interesting details in the church are paintings of Prince Leopold and Princess Charlotte, and a clock with cannon balls for weights, raised by a little capstan*. The mother of Jane and Anna Maria Porter is buried in the churchyard. The three women removed to Esher in 1803, after Jane had published *Thaddeus of Warsaw*, the novel praised by the great Polish patriot, Kościuszko. It was at Esher that Jane Porter wrote *The Scottish Chiefs*, and Anna Maria wrote *The Hungarian Brothers* and *The Knight of St John*, the latter of which was the last book read aloud by Prince Leopold to Princess Charlotte, the day before her death. The site of the cottage in which the Porters lived until the death of their mother in 1831 is now occupied by 85 High Street. Their brother, Sir Robert Ker Porter, whose career was as romantic as it was distinguished, painted an altarpiece which he gave to St George's Church.

Esher's most cherished possession, the tree-shaded green, is neighboured by Christ Church, which was rebuilt in 1854 when it superseded St George's as the parish church. It still has thirteenth-century details, a seventeenth-century brass, and memorials to Prince Leopold, Duke of Albany, who died in 1884, and Leopold, King of the Belgians.

Montague Phillips, who was organist of Christ Church for many years before his death in 1969, composed a *Surrey Suite* for orchestra, but the best-known of his many compositions is undoubtedly *The Rebel Maid*, which is still a popular production for amateur operatic societies. His wife, Clara Butterworth, who created the leading role of Lady Mary Trefusis, and is also nostalgically remembered by the older generation of theatre-goers in *The Lilac Domino*, and for her enchanting 'Lili' in *Lilac Time*, still lives in Esher.

On the far side of the green are the brick gatehouse lodges to the Esher estate, which occupies the greater part of the site of Esher Place. Originally a palace built on low ground beside the River Mole by Bishop Wayneflete of Winchester in 1470, it was repaired by Cardinal Wolsey, who retired there when deprived of the Great Seal. He complained that the low situation made him feel ill, and was allowed to move to Richmond. All that remains of the palace is the great fifteenth-century gatehouse, sometimes referred to as Wayneflete's Tower and sometimes as Wolsey's Tower. The house and grounds laid out by Henry Pelham, described by Thomson in *The Seasons* as:

---

* It is now wound by electricity.

Esher's groves
There in the sweetest solitude, embrac'd
By the soft windings of the gentle Mole
From courts and senate Pelham found repose

have now disappeared under the housing estate, but the curious stone seat he built, called The Traveller's Rest, can be seen beside the entrance to the Sandown Race Course, opposite the handsome eighteenth-century Sandown House, on the Portsmouth Road.

The present Esher Place, built for the first Viscount D'Abernon in 'French Pavilion' style, with a sunk garden by Lutyens, is now used by the Electrical Trades Union as a college and convalescent home.

Across the River Mole is Wayland's Farm, on the site of the farm where William Duckett the Elder, inventor of the drill plough, lived, and was visited by George III. The King sent Duckett's son, William Duckett the Younger, to the settlement at Cape Town to introduce his father's system and implements of agriculture.

Rosebriars, in Esher Park Avenue, is the home of Mr R. C. Sherriff, author of *Journey's End*, *Badger's Green* and other successful plays. He frequently opens his garden to the public in aid of charities.

The eighteenth-century Friends' Meeting House is passed in Claremont Lane (A244) which gives access to the housing estate now covering part of the park of Claremont, and continues through the modern residential area of Oxshott to Leatherhead.

The original house on the site of Claremont was built by Sir John Vanbrugh, but he sold it about seven years later to the statesman, Thomas Pelham, later Duke of Newcastle, who gave it the name of Claremont. He sold it to Lord Clive, and Vanbrugh's house was replaced by the present building, designed by Lancelot Brown, and his partner, Henry Holland, the former of whom also remodelled the garden.

It is sometimes said that Claremont 'saw much tragedy', which is undeniable, but it also saw much happiness, for Princess Charlotte spent what was probably the happiest year of her short life there, with her adored husband Prince Leopold of Saxe-Coburg, before her death in childbirth, and Queen Victoria loved to visit 'Uncle

9 (opposite above) *Royal Holloway College, Egham, from the south-west*

10 (opposite below) *Horsley Towers*

Leopold' at Claremont before he accepted the throne of Belgium. She gave it to her youngest son, Leopold, Duke of Albany, on his marriage to Princess Helena of Waldeck in 1882, and it also proved a quiet refuge for more than one dethroned European monarch and his family. It is now a Christian Science School for Girls, and is open to the public at advertised times.

Claremont's woods and lake, formerly part of the Park, are now owned by the National Trust, and are open to the public daily during the greater part of daylight hours. The entrance is on the Portsmouth Road, which continues through open country across Fairmile Common to Cobham, made up of Street Cobham, which is almost entirely modern and split by the main road, Church Cobham and Cobham Tilt on the A245 to Leatherhead, which turns off on the left beside the White Hart, a fine old coaching inn which has known many notable travellers. The Leatherhead road changes its name six times before it reaches Leatherhead, and the first portion, between Street Cobham and Church Cobham, is known appropriately as 'Between Streets'.

Relics of the Bronze and Iron Ages have been found at Leigh Hill, north of Church Cobham, and although the village is being invaded by newcomers, the modern houses are attractive, and numerous old houses survive. Church Street, which is now a one-way street, and cannot be entered by traffic from the High Street, is particularly redolent of the past. Church Stile House, beside the lich-gate, dates from 1432, although restored in 1635, and is neighboured by scarcely less ancient houses.

St Andrew's Church has been much restored, but has a mainly Norman tower and Early English work in the chancel and north chapel, but its chief interest is in its monuments, particularly a palimpsest brass of 1500, and a tiny brass of the same date which is said to be the only representation in England of the Nativity on a brass. Unfortunately when I revisited the church on an afternoon in 1974 it was locked, and although a notice said the key was available at a nearby house, there was no reply to my knocking.

In the churchyard is the ostentatious memorial to Harvey Combe, who died in 1818, and his family. A more impressive mausoleum is to be found on the far side of the cemetery in Cobham Tilt, where Sir

73

Robert MacAlpine, the great road-builder, who died in 1939, lies with his family behind the massive gates of a plain concrete mausoleum beside the River Mole.

Cobham Lodge, a white-painted Regency house in Cobham Park Road, was the home of Caroline Molesworth for half a century. Her *Cobham Journals* were published in 1880, and summarize her observations of weather conditions and plant life for a period of 44 years. Her collection of dried plants was sent to Kew.

Cobham High Street is followed by Mill Road (still the A245), where the best-known group of Cobham's older houses stands north of a curve in the river. Unfortunately, the mill has been demolished, but Ham Manor dates from the early eighteenth century and Cedar House from the fifteenth century. The latter was altered and enlarged in the seventeenth and eighteenth centuries. It was given to the National Trust in 1938.

Woodlands, which stood at the corner of Fairmile Lane and Green Lane, was the home of Mrs C. W. Earle, granddaughter of Thomas Villiers, first Earl of Clarendon, and she was visited there by Burne-Jones and Henry James, among others. She was well-known in the nineteenth century social and horticultural circles for her books *Pot Pourri from a Surrey Garden* and *More Potpourri from a Surrey Garden*. They are aptly named, for they deal with many matters besides gardening, but they both still find a place in the library of every collector of gardening books. Their slightly period style does not detract from their common sense and her surprisingly modern outlook, particularly in regard to the bringing up of children. She died in 1925, and the house has been demolished, but Mr David Taylor, a local historian of Cobham, tells me a part of the garden has been incorporated in that of another house. Earle's Wood, off Fairmile Lane, was named after Mrs Earle.

Mill Road is followed by Stoke Road, which passes the little Plough Inn beside the turning to Cobham and Stoke D'Abernon Station, which in true country fashion, is as far as possible from the places it serves. Beyond is the tree-lined road to Stoke D'Abernon church, turning off on the west.

Evidence of very early human occupation has been found at Stoke D'Abernon, near the parish church of St Mary the Virgin, and Roman

74

and Saxon work are incorporated in the building. There is no recognizable village centre, and the church and manor-house stand well away from other buildings and modern development. The church is one of the very few actually on the banks of the Mole, and although it has been over-restored, it is full of interest, with ancient stained glass, an elaborately carved Jacobean pulpit, with its sounding board and hour-glass, a notable oak chest dating from 1210, traces of thirteenth-century wall paintings, and a bell cast about 1450 by the famous woman bell-founder, Joanna Sturdy of Croydon, which is still sound. Above all, there is a magnificent array of monuments illustrating in brass and stone the changes of ownership of the manor, which passed by marriage from the D'Abernons in turn to the Norburys, Brays and Vincents.

The brasses include the oldest brass in England, commemorating Sir John D'Abernon, who died in 1277. It is over 6 feet in length, and a wonderful example of the engraver's art, depicting Sir John in armour, with his feet resting on a lion which is engagingly biting his lance. His son, also Sir John, who died in 1327, has a slightly smaller and less perfectly drawn brass.

The Norbury Chapel was added in 1490 by Sir John Norbury, who had fought at Bosworth Field. It incorporates a fireplace, which is unusual in a pre-Reformation church. It has such a range of brasses and monuments of both historical and artistic interest that it is impossible to mention them all here, and the reader must be referred to the guides available in the church, which give a choice between an excellent illustrated short guide, and a more detailed and technical reprint from *The Archaeological Journal*, Vol. cxviii by Mr C. A. Ralegh Radford.

The earliest known rector, who lived in the thirteenth century, is commemorated in the church by a Norman-French inscription.

Sarah, daughter of the Rev. Thomas Neasham, who was rector for 32 years, married George Jeffreys in 1667. Seymour Schofield, in his biography *Jeffreys of the Bloody Assizes*, refutes the frequently repeated story that she was the servant of an heiress, and that Jeffreys married her after she had been turned out on the streets penniless by the irate father of the heiress, upon whose fortune Jeffreys had his eye. Schofield states that Sarah was able to bring a 'portion' to her marriage, even if it was only a modest one, and that it was a love match. She died after only 10 years, but before her death he was knighted and elected a Bencher of the Inner Temple, and her life with him was a happy one. She was spared the knowledge of the odium he was to incur after the Monmouth Rebellion.

The present manor-house of Stoke D'Abernon, delightfully situated east of the church in a bend of the River Mole, dates chiefly from 1757, but incorporates part of a sixteenth-century house. It is believed to be the last of a series of earlier houses going back to a Roman villa with a bath house, the remains of which lie below the lawns fronting the terrace.

One of these earlier houses had the romantic distinction of being the first of which there is an actual record that it was lent for a honeymoon. The powerful William Marshal won the hand of Isabella (or Eva) de Clare, heiress of the Earls of Pembroke, in 1189. The story of their marriage and subsequent honeymoon at the country estate of Sir Enguerrand D'Abernon is told in a poetical biography of the bridegroom, *L'Histoire de Guillaume le Maréschal*, which was discovered and edited by Paul Meyer for the Société de l'Histoire de France, and retold by J. H. Round in *The Ancestor*.

A later occupant of the manor-house was Canon F. P. Phillips, who was a grandson of the Duc D'Orléans—Philippe Égalité. He lived there for nearly 70 years, for 40 of which he was rector. His successor was the Rev. Henry Noel Waldegrave, who became eleventh Earl of Waldegrave in 1933, on the death of his nephew. He was then 79, and died three years later.

The house now belongs to the Inner London Education Authority.

The 'Stoke Moran' of Conan Doyle's famous story, *The Speckled Band*, which was 'four miles from Leatherhead' has been identified by some as Stoke D'Abernon manor-house, but as all devotees of the Sherlock Holmes stories know, there is a great disparity between Watson's description of the house, and the reality. One commentator tried to remedy the discrepancy by saying that it was a mansion 'since demolished' nearby. However, there appears to be no record of such a house, and either Watson was being deliberately misleading, or he was suffering from one of his well-known lapses of memory.

Just beyond Stoke D'Abernon bridge is Slyfield Manor, a large seventeenth-century brick building incorporating part of a larger timber-framed late medieval house, which can be seen clearly from the road. Slyfield Farm, on the north, was originally part of the service wing of the seventeenth-century house.

The Slyfields were a Surrey family who crop up in several neighbouring villages. The will of Edmund Slyfield, who became Sheriff of Surrey and Sussex in the reign of Elizabeth I, is of special interest to local and social historians, for it lists his bequests of clothing and other items to his 16 sons and daughters in great detail, adding some rather sour comments on his eldest daughter, Elizabeth, who was left £40, with the admonition that she was not to 'troble molest or disquiett my saide wyfe, her mother, my Executrix'.

Edmund's son and successor was a spendthrift, who was forced to sell Slyfield, which was bought by the Shiers in 1614. The present house was built by George Shiers, whose grandson, Sir George Shiers, was a great benefactor to a number of Surrey villages, including Great Bookham, where Slyfields and Shiers are buried.

Almost opposite Slyfield Manor is the entrance to the Yehudi Menuhin School of Music, set in a quiet park beside the River Mole. Founded in 1963 as a co-educational boarding school for children who show promise as musicians, it has already attracted grants from the Gulbenkian and other foundations, and in 1974 was accorded, along with the Royal Ballet School, a special status as a centre of education for the performing arts. The happy, healthy and delightfully well mannered youngsters have taken part in concerts at the Fairfield Hall, Croydon, and the main concert halls in London, and the Windsor Festival, and have gone on to win scholarships and prizes at the Royal Schools of Music in London, and Conservatoires abroad.

There is a choice of routes from here: to continue south-east along the Cobham Road to Fetcham; rejoin the A245 to Leatherhead, or return to the Portsmouth Road (A3), turning left at the White Lion. Just before Cobham Bridge on the A3 is 'Matthew Arnold Close', on the site of the cottage in which Matthew Arnold spent the last years of his life, calling himself the 'Hermit of the Mole', and his wife the 'Hermitess'.

A plaque on the bridge over the River Mole, seldom noticed by passers-by, commemorates the tradition that the first bridge there was built by Queen Matilda, wife of Henry I, about 1100, after one of her maidens had been drowned crossing the ford. The bridge was rebuilt in 1743 and widened on the north side in 1914.

Beyond the bridge is the entrance to Painshill Park, which was bought in 1738 by the Hon. Charles Hamilton, who converted the grounds into a landscaped park embellished with an astonishing number of grottoes, temples, ruins and follies, to the admiration of all eighteenth-century visitors, although the Gothic Temple was severely criticized by Walpole, who commented 'Goths never built summer-houses or temples in a garden', but who admired everything else he saw there. 'Liberty' Wilkes strolled in the park 'like the first solitary man through Paradise', and John Wesley, who visited 'Cobham Gardens' in 1779 and 1790, thought they far exceeded the 'celebrated gardens at Stow . . .'. The park was especially famous for its trees. A Cedar of Lebanon, said to be the largest in England, greatly impressed Carl von Linné, son of the famous naturalist, when he visited the park in the company of Sir Joseph Banks.

Hamilton even installed a real live hermit in the 'Hermitage'. The hermit was promised £700 on condition that he slept on a mat, never spoke a word, and neglected his toilet, with the result he threw up his post in three weeks, and could not be replaced. Not surprisingly, Hamilton's expensive hobby eventually made him a bankrupt.

The house was rebuilt in 1778 and remodelled by Decimus Burton about 1840. It has now been divided into self-contained flats. Great efforts are still being made by Cobham residents to save the house and what is left of the park from further destruction. Mr David Taylor has kept me in touch with the various projects, which have included a film of the park shown on the BBC *Nationwide* programme, and inclusion in an exhibition at the Victoria and Albert Museum dealing with country houses and parks. In October 1974 he was able to report the purchase of the first 40 acres of the park by the Elmbridge District Council. The remaining 160 acres have yet to be acquired, but it is hoped the acquisition of the whole will be one of Britain's contributions to the European Architectural Heritage Year in 1975.

At the Painshill roundabout the road turns sharp left to run between the woodlands of birch, oak and Scots pine of Wisley Common and Ockham Common—one of the loveliest stretches of the Portsmouth Road. Bolder Mere glints through the trees on Ockham Common shortly before the well-signposted turning to the Royal Horticultural Garden on the right.

The Garden originated in the 1870s when 66 acres were bought by George F. Wilson of Weybridge, a skilled amateur gardener who was at one time Treasurer of the Royal Horticultural Society. Only a small area was planted in the early days, when Wilson developed an oak wood as a Wild Garden, and also built a small rock garden and a series of ponds. Miss Jekyll took such a keen interest in the enterprise that she was gratified at being allowed to do 'actual spade work with him', and helped to lay the stones of the rock garden. In her book *Wood and Garden* she says she particularly admired and envied the *Primula denticulata* there, which she was unable to grow with such success in the sandier soil of her own garden at Munstead. Wilson cultivated an amazing number and variety of plants in a comparatively small area, and Miss Jekyll comments: 'I take it to be about the most instructive [garden] it is possible to see.'

After Wilson's death in 1902, the ground was purchased by Sir Thomas Hanbury, owner of the famous garden at La Mortola, Ventimiglia, Italy, and given by him to the Royal Horticultural Society 'for the purpose of an Experimental Garden, and the Encouragement and Improvement of Scientific and Practical Horticulture in all its branches'—a rather dull-sounding objective which gives little hint of the beauty which has been achieved, while faithfully carrying out the primary object of the scientific side of the garden.

When the Society moved from its Chiswick Garden, which it had occupied for over 80 years, in the Centenary year of 1904, only 19 of the 66 acres had been cultivated. The Council insisted that the woodland garden must be 'carefully preserved and continued'.

Following the stimulus given to rock-gardening by the publication in 1907 of Reginald Farrer's *My Rock Garden*, the original small rock garden was extended and landscaped into the splendid rock garden there today. Many of the plants were given by Sir Frank Crisp, of

Friar Park, near Henley, and by A. E. Bowles from his famous garden at Myddelton House, near Enfield.

The wrought-iron entrance gates to Wisley Garden are a memorial to the Rev. W. Wilkes, the Secretary whose energy and vision helped to rescue the Society from the verge of bankruptcy in 1888 to ever-increasing prosperity and world status before his retirement in 1920. Wilkes was a notable 'character', who was successively curate of Croydon and Vicar of Shirley. He maintained a garden at Shirley which he called 'The Wilderness', in which he developed the popular Shirley Poppy from the field poppy *Papaver rhoeas*. Under his influence several of his congregation became interested in gardening and joined the staff of the Royal Horticultural Society, the most widely known of whom is undoubtedly the beloved nonagenarian broadcaster, Mr Fred Streeter, who was born in Shirley. Wilkes died in 1923, and the gates at Wisley incorporate his initials and stylized Shirley Poppies. Other memorials to famous gardeners are described in the excellent guide to Wisley, which has many coloured illustrations.

Although special facilities are, naturally, extended to the Fellows of the Society, the garden, which now covers over 200 acres, is open to the general public.

On leaving Wisley, it is well worthwhile to turn left and make a détour through the fields and water-meadows, to see the little Norman churches of Wisley and Pyrford, which have so happily escaped the hands of 'restorers', and retain all their original simplicity and charm. Both these churches date from the middle of the twelfth century.

The road to Pyrford Church crosses the River Wey, and takes an abrupt turn over the Wey Navigation Canal at the point where the Anchor Inn is set beside the water, to tempt mariners and motorists. There is frequently a trim motor cruiser or rowing boat moored alongside to complete a very attractive picture.

St Nicholas's is set on a low knoll from which the roofless grey walls of Newark Priory can be seen through the trees, but the neighbouring mill was burned to the ground in 1966.

Pyrford church has the additional interest of wall-paintings as old as the church itself, with another layer dating from about 1200. The earlier paintings have mounted horsemen and a row of men wearing conical hats and carrying staves, not found in wall-paintings elsewhere, but resembling the carvings of Norman soldiers at Kikpeck in Herefordshire and Barfreston in Kent.

There is a modern mural in the porch depicting a highly imaginative 'history', but a more reliable account of the parish is given in the guidebook in the church.

A dug-out canoe discovered in 1926 led to the uncovering of the site of a prehistoric village of about 2500 BC near Pyrford Lock. The relics are now in the Weybridge Museum. There are a number of other prehistoric sites in the neighbourhood, including a fine barrow on Wisley Common, and the Pyrford Stone, just south of Pyrford Church. The circular churchyard of Pyrford Church suggests a Celtic origin.

The older houses and cottages at Pyrford date chiefly from the sixteenth century, when Pyrford Place was the home of Sir John Wolley, Latin Secretary to Elizabeth I, and his wife, Elizabeth, the eldest daughter of William More of Loseley. She was Lady-in-Waiting to the Queen, who visited Pyrford Place. When their niece, Ann More, married the poet John Donne, against her father's wishes, the young couple took refuge at Pyrford with Sir Francis Wolley, who had succeeded to the estate.

Denzil Onslow bought the manor in 1677. John Evelyn records on 23 August 1681 that he was 'invited to Mr Denzil Onslow's at his seat at Purford (*sic*) where there was much company, and such an extraordinary feast, as I had hardly seen at any country gentleman's table. What made it more remarkable was that there was not anything save what his estate about it affords; as venison, rabbits, hares, pheasants, partridges, pigeons, quails, poultry, all sorts of fowl in season from his own decoy near his house, and all sorts of fresh fish. After dinner, we went to see sport at the decoy, where I never saw so many herons. The seat stands in a flat, the ground pasture rarely watered and exceedingly improved since Mr Onslow bought it . . . the house is timber, but commodious, with one ample dining room . . .' The house was demolished by Robert, Lord Onslow in 1776, but the summer house has been preserved.

Pyrford is extending north to join the modern suburbs of Byfleet, the older part of which dates back at least to Norman times, when it was known as Biflet. The manor was owned by the Crown and visited by various English kings. The ghost of Anne of Denmark, wife of James I, and of a dwarf, are said to haunt the seventeenth-century manor-house beside the Wey.

The thirteenth-century church of St Mary has wall-paintings and interesting memorials, including a brass to Thomas Tyler, a rector who died in 1454. Stephen Duck, a Wiltshire labourer who attracted the attention of Queen Caroline, wife of George II, with his poetry, became Rector of Byfleet in 1752, but two years later drowned himself in the Thames in a fit of melancholy.

George Smith, the publisher who founded the *Dictionary of National Biography*, was buried in the churchyard in 1901.

The road running south to rejoin the Portsmouth Road at the south-western end of Ripley passes close to the ruins of Newark Priory, which was built for Augustinian canons about 50 years after Pyrford Church. It was here that Thomas Love Peacock used to meet his sweetheart, Fanny Falkner, to whom he was engaged in the summer of 1807. The engagement was broken off by the inter-ference of a third person. Fanny, supposing herself deserted, married another man, and died in 1808, but Peacock always cherished the memory of his first love.

Ripley High Street cries out for a by-pass. As it is a part of the old coach road, it can never have been completely peaceful, but before the Second World War, when I first knew it, Ripley did not have to contend with the nightmare of present-day traffic thundering through it continuously. The wonder is that it is still so attractive, with trees lining the greater part of the wide High Street, and many sixteenth-, seventeenth- and eighteenth-century buildings remaining. The most notable are Ride House, the Old Manor House, Cedar House (formerly the George Inn), and the half-timbered many-gabled Anchor Inn. It was in one of the numerous inns of 'the pretty little village of Ripley' that Sherlock Holmes spent a day, before returning to the 'detached house' near Woking Station to unmask the odious Harrison in *The Naval Treaty*.

Behind the High Street, and unsuspected by those who speed through Ripley, is the long, wedge-shaped village green, which must surely be the refuge from the traffic's roar which keeps the inhabitants sane. The cricket club dates from the eighteenth century and helps to preserve the peaceful village atmosphere so conspicuously lacking in the High Street. West of the green is Dunsborough Park, the garden of which, with its rose valley, tropical plants and rare shrubs, is open to the public several times a year.

Ripley church was mentioned in a document of 1549, in which it was called a chantry chapel 'builded long time past for an hospital and sithen altered, unto which the parishioners dwelling here have used for their own ease to resort to hear Divine Service . . .'. It was almost entirely rebuilt in the mid-nineteenth century, but some Norman work survives, including a beautifully carved string course below the level of the chancel windows, which is unlike any other twelfth-century work in Surrey.

In the early days of the pedal cycling craze, Ripley was the goal of London cycling clubs. Not only was it a convenient 'run', but the Dibble family at the Anchor Inn gave the cyclists a warm welcome, when they were barred from many 'respectable' hotels. Charles Harper, in *Cycling Round London*, says: '. . . cycles [were] stacked by the hundred in the village street on Saturdays and Sundays in the 1870s. Among the first comers were the very early racing cyclists, including Cortis, the Hon. Ion Keith Falconer and Jack Keen'. Their cycling friends subscribed for a memorial window in Ripley church to Annie and Harriet Dibble, and to Cortis.

There are some delightful old houses and cottages in Rose Lane, which borders the south-western end of Ockham Park, and continues to West Horsley.

Ockham Park, which has changed hands many times down the centuries, was bought by Peter King, who became Lord Chancellor in 1725 and was created Lord King. His descendants became Earls of Lovelace. They lived at Ockham Park, exercising an autocratic supervision over the building of the cottages in the village. Part of the mansion was destroyed by fire, and the eighteenth-century stables and orangery have been converted into flats. Ockham Park is now the property of a private company.

The thirteenth-century parish church, on the verge of the park, has memorials to the Lovelace family. The east window is famous for its thirteenth-century glass, and there is the earliest known brass in Surrey in memory of a priest. On the outside of one of the chancel windows is scratched the inscription 'W. Peters New leaded this in 1772 and Never was paid for the Same'.

William de Ockham or Occam, the fourteenth-century 'Doctor Invincibilis', is believed to have been a native of Ockham. He was a formidable controversialist who accused two successive Popes of heresy—and survived! His voluminous writings on theology, politics, philosophy and logic are said to have influenced Luther in formulating his doctrines.

Nicholas of Occam or Hotham, who flourished about 1280, a Franciscan monk whose works are mentioned by Leland, was also presumably born at Ockham.

After Ripley the Portsmouth Road bends south, with turnings on the left to Send Marsh and Send. St Mary's Church, Send, and the eighteenth-century Send Grove, are beautifully situated near the River Wey, at a considerable distance from the overspill of Woking's housing developments in the north of the parish. Although the church was badly damaged by fire in 1965, it has been carefully restored. Fortunately, the early sixteenth-century brass of Laurence and Alys Slyfield escaped damage.

St Edward's Roman Catholic church is near the site of a hunting lodge belonging to Edward the Confessor. The church owns a chasuble with a view of Sutton Place embroidered on it by the ladies of Henry VIII's Court. Buried in the church is Maude Valerie White, the composer of hundreds of songs. Among the lyrics she set to music were poems by Herrick, Browning and Victor Hugo. She received a Civil List pension for her services to music, until her death in 1937.

The manor of Woking belonged to the Crown from Norman times until the eighteenth century, but when Defoe saw Woking in 1796 it was still only a small market town. Little was left of old Woking after the A247 was widened for modern traffic needs. St Peter's Church has some Norman fabric, Perpendicular windows and a thirteenth-century chancel. The gallery is Jacobean, and there are some plain late medieval pews, sixteenth-century brasses, and seventeenth- and eighteenth-century monuments. Old Hall beside the Wey was a favourite palace of the Tudors, of which nothing is left but an overgrown moated site and some of the foundations.

Modern Woking developed at spectacular speed after the coming of the railway in 1838. Outstanding among much undistinguished building is the Shah Jehan Mosque, built in 1889 in the grounds of the Oriental Institute, and now the headquarters of the British Muslim Society.

It was at Woking that the remarkable Ockenden Venture, which has done such splendid work in the relief of refugees, was started in 1951, at Ockenden House, White Rose Lane, the home of Miss Joan Pearce, a native of Woking.

The main entrance gates of Sutton Place, in the south-west of the large and scattered parish of Send, are beside the Portsmouth Road, on the outskirts of Guildford. The house is one of the outstanding Tudor mansions of England and is encircled on three sides by the River Wey, which runs through the extensive park.

Sir Richard Weston was granted the estate in 1521, the year after he had attended Henry VIII to the Field of the Cloth of Gold. The name of the architect is unknown, but it has been conjectured that the great use made of terra cotta indicates an Italian influence. Sir Richard was always high in the favour of the King, who visited him at Sutton Place in 1533. Many tributes have been paid to the abilities of Sir Richard as a statesman and diplomat, but he must have had a very curious and complex character to remain in the King's service after the execution of his only son in 1536, on a suspicion of an intrigue with Anne Boleyn. He was succeeded at Sutton Place by his grandson, Sir Henry, who entertained Elizabeth I there for three days in 1591.

Sir Richard's skill in diplomacy must have been inherited by his descendant and namesake, Sir Richard Weston, who contrived to live through the Civil War unscathed. He inherited Sutton Place and Clandon in 1613, and left a lasting benefit to the locality by constructing the Wey Navigation Canal connecting Guildford and Weybridge. He used the Dutch system of locks to cut off the many eccentric bends in the River Wey. He also established a new system of rotation of crops based on the cultivation of clover, flax and turnips, which he had seen in practice in Flanders.

It was probably due to the expense he incurred in cutting the canal that he was forced to sell West Clandon to Sir Richard Onslow in 1641. He died in 1652 before the canal was completed, but the work was carried on by his son John, and the canal was opened in 1653.

Subsequently, as Frederick Harrison says in *Annals of an Old Manor House, Sutton Place, Guildford*, the Westons 'not only disappear from the annals of England, but they are hardly traceable in the annals of the county. They mind their lands beside the Wey, nor think of adding a brick to the old place that was now too large for their estate.'

In the first 17 years of this century, Sutton Place, after a long period of neglect, was leased to the newspaper magnate, Alfred Harmsworth, Lord Northcliffe, who spent over £70,000 on its restoration.

The guests at Lady Northcliffe's Sunday luncheon parties reflect the extraordinary diversity of Northcliffe's interests. Naturally there were many politicians, but among others were Paderewski, Selous, the big game hunter (said to be the original of Rider Haggard's *Allan Quatermain*), H. B. Irving, Gervase Elwes, the singer, Alfred Lyttelton, the county cricketer, and Graham White, the aeronaut. Major Baden-Powell, brother of the Chief Scout, conducted scientific experiments at Sutton Place, with the help and encouragement of Northcliffe, and fixed up a wireless telephone there before they became generally known and installed.

By 1917, Northcliffe tired of the luxury of Sutton Place, and longed for the comforts of Elmwood, always his best-loved home. He accepted an offer from the Duke of Sutherland for the remainder of his lease of Sutton Place, satisfied with having 'helped to perpetuate a beautiful thing' by restoring it to all its former glory.

Sutton Place is now the home of Mr Paul Getty, the American multi-millionaire, who also took it over after a period of neglect, and spent much time, money, and informed good taste in restoring it as a perfect setting for part of his collection of art treasures.

A striking feature of the superb gardens, which command views of the North Downs, is formal clipped yew hedges enclosing a whole series of huge rectangles, thickly planted in spring with yellow and white narcissi, in contrast to the natural woodlands, interplanted with flowering shrubs, on the slopes dropping down to the River Wey. There seems to be no record of the planting of the yew hedges, but they were certainly there in the time of the Northcliffes, and probably far earlier, as they look exactly the same in photographs taken in 1909, in my possession, as they do now. There, too, are the formal pool and the beautifully kept lawns.

The gardens are open to the public at advertised times, and more rarely, the house is open in aid of local charities.

The North Downs

The well-wooded North Downs rise gently from the northern plain, but have a steep escarpment overlooking the Weald. They run at an almost unvarying height of 600 to 800 feet, broken only by the valleys of the Wey and Mole.

The prehistoric trackways, of which by far the oldest and most important were the Hoar, or Harrow Way, and the Old Road, or so-called 'Pilgrims' Way' follow the high southern edge.

It is impossible in a book dealing with the whole of Surrey to follow the line of the Old Road and its deviations in detail, or to enter into a full discussion of the popular name of 'The Pilgrims' Way', a title which did not appear before the eighteenth century. There are almost as many opinions on the exact line of the 53½ miles of the Old Road in Surrey as there are books about it, each author arguing passionately in favour of his own conjectures. The most readable of all books written on the subject is Hilaire Belloc's breezy and dogmatic *The Old Road*, but for practical purposes, the best to date are *The Pilgrims' Way*, by Séan Jennett, and *A Guide to the Pilgrims' Way and North Downs Way* by Christopher John Wright.

The North Downs Way, which sometimes merges with the Old Road, and sometimes strikes out on its own to take in some special view point, is one of the long-distance footpaths established by the Countryside Commission. It runs for 121 miles from Winchester to the Kentish Coast, but at present only the Surrey section is open fully.

The nearest routes from London to the North Downs are from Croydon, Sanderstead or Sutton.

Farleigh, only just over the Surrey border, was included in the Croydon boundary when it became a London Borough, but fought so vigorously against incorporation in Greater London that it remains

12 (opposite) *Part of the south front of Loseley House*

an unspoiled rural village. It has a gem of a church, almost entirely Norman, with windows not later than 1250, and a delightful fifteenth-century brass. The story of Farleigh's successful fight to retain its individuality is told in Vol. VIII of the *Local History Records* of the Bourne Society, as an inspiration to communities similarly threatened.

Farleigh is the most northerly of the towns and villages which lie between the Kentish border and the A25 from London to Eastbourne. Chelsham, south of Farleigh, has a common, a school, three inns and some scattered houses, but no real village. The church is over a mile away. It was formerly midway between three old houses, Ledgers, Fairchildes and Chelsham Court manor-house, but all three are partially or wholly demolished, and the church alone is left, seemingly unreasonably far from the village, but actually almost the centre of its sparsely inhabited parish of some 4,000 acres. The chief possession of the church is a richly carved screen, originally considerably larger than today. There is also the unusual feature of the Royal Arms of HM Queen Elizabeth II, painted by Marjorie Wratton and set up by the parishioners during Coronation Year. The 'Kelly' Bible and Prayer Book are a reminder of Thomas Kelly, a native of Chelsham, who tended his father's sheep on Scotshall Farm, went to London in 1786 at the age of 14, with only a few shillings in his pocket, made a fortune as a publisher and became Lord Mayor of London in 1836. He is buried in the churchyard.

Warlingham, over 600 feet above Caterham Valley, has a restored thirteenth-century church with a fifteenth-century wall painting of St Christopher, but its proudest claim to fame is that it was here the Prayer Book authorized by Edward VI was first used, and its compiler, Archbishop Cranmer, was present at the service. In our own day, it had the first church service ever televised. Chelsham also has a vicarage and almshouses dating from the seventeenth century, and an attractive old inn.

Between Warlingham and Woldingham is the curiously named and enchanting Halliloo or Hallelu Valley, which the Nature Conservancy has declared a site of Special Scientific Importance.

Woldingham's disused chapel of St Agatha is high on the Downs. St Paul's, a mile to the north, was built in 1933 at the expense of

Lord Craigmyle, as a memorial to his father-in-law, Lord Inchcape of the P. & O. Line. There are good stained glass windows by Douglas Strachan, and a text in the apse is set with agates, 300 of which were sent by the Nizam of Hyderabad for the purpose.

A large area of the parish is in Green Belt country, and Marden House is in an outstandingly lovely park of great beech and chestnut trees. The older house was destroyed by fire in 1879, and the rebuilt house is now a convent. Evelyn records in his diary, under the date 12 October 1677, that he accompanied Sir Robert Clayton to Marden 'an estate he had bought lately of my kinsman, Sir John Evelyn of Godstone in Surrey, which from a despicable farmhouse Sir Robert had erected into a seat with extraordinary expense. It is in such solitude among hills as, being not above 16 miles from London, seems almost incredible, the ways up to it are so winding and intricate.'

The National Trust owns large areas of the Downs, and when Sir Adrian Boult was living at South Hawke in 1958, he bought 44 acres of fields and gave covenants over them to the National Trust, to preserve the view from his house. The fields now form part of the golf course, and are safe from development.

Titsey Place, hidden behind trees, was largely rebuilt in the eighteenth century by Sir John Gresham, the eighth and last baronet, who also removed the old church in the park, and transferred its Gresham memorials to a new church beside the road. There are later memorials to the Leveson-Gower family. Granville Leveson-Gower excavated the site of a Roman villa in the park in 1864, and a Romano-Celtic temple was excavated in 1879 in Church Field, near the line of the old London–Brighton road.

Tatsfield's little Norman church is close to the Old Road, well away from the village, and is chiefly notable for the magnificent view from the churchyard, far over Kent, Surrey and Sussex. Tatsfield is the most easterly of Surrey's Downland villages, and it is only a mile and a half along the Old Road, here clearly defined, from the Kentish border.

Caterham, like so many Downland towns, originated in a village clustering round a Norman church on the hilltop, with the newer development in the valley, which was virtually uninhabited before the coming of the railway.

The wooded hills are so steep that in places hand rails have been provided for those who go on foot, and there are many splendid viewpoints. The Roman road ran high up on the side of the valley, and the valley town was also by-passed by the modern Eastbourne road (A22) which runs along the eastern hilltops to Godstone Hill. Three-quarters of the area of Caterham is in the Green Belt, and it includes the viewpoint of Gravelly Hill, near the line of the Old Road and the North Downs Way.

Chaldon lies west of Caterham, close to the southern boundary of Croydon. The small parish church of SS Peter and Paul, high on the edge of Farthing Down, has one of the most important wall paintings in England. Dating from 1200, it has a rare combination of the Last Judgment and the Ladder of Salvation, and is crowded with figures on a dark red background, completely covering the west wall. The pulpit was one of the few made during the Commonwealth, and there are some unusual epitaphs.

Banstead, west of the Brighton road (A23) and the proposed M23, is now a sizeable town, but it has its roots in prehistoric times, and was first mentioned in a Saxon charter of AD 987 as 'Benestede', which is said to mean 'bean farm'. Banstead church was given to Southwark monastery in the reign of Henry I, and later the manor was the property of Hugh de Burgh, the illustrious soldier-statesman, who died at his Banstead home in 1345. His son sold the manor to Edward I.

The name of the Mint Arms, and of Mint Farm, off Park Road, is a reminder that peppermint has been grown commercially in the area since the Middle Ages, just as the Woolpack Inn is a reminder that Banstead was an important centre of the wool trade. The sheep on Banstead Downs were especially noted for the high quality of their wool and mutton, but with the diminution of the wool trade, the Downs became more famous for the horse races, which were watched by Charles II in 1683. When the races were transferred to Epsom Downs, Banstead developed as a residential district.

All Saints Church dates from the late twelfth century, and has an octagonal Perpendicular font, a tablet dated 1618 of a baby in a chrisom robe, and several eighteenth-century monuments.

Woodmansterne, on the east of Banstead, is referred to in Domesday

Book as Odemerestor, said to be 'the thorn bush close to the forest'. The Lamberts, whose memorials are in Banstead church, lived there from the fourteenth century. Woodmansterne's Norman church has been rebuilt, and hardly anything remains of the original fabric.

Chipstead, south-east of Banstead, was owned by Chertsey Abbey from Saxon times until the Dissolution. The thirteenth-century church has a transept rebuilt by the Rev. P. Aubertin, who became rector in 1809 and is buried in the church. He did all the necessary repairs, acting as his own architect, and even painted the stained glass in the windows. Among the monuments is one to Sir Edward Banks, who died in 1835. He started life as a railway navvy, became a wealthy contractor, and carried out Rennie's designs for 'the three noblest bridges in the world'—Waterloo, Southwark and London.

Chipstead developed when the Chipstead Valley line was built in the 1890s. The line was not extended to Tattenham Corner until 1901. There are still a number of seventeenth-century farms and cottages in the neighbourhood.

Burgh Heath, which is cut in two by the A217 to Brighton, has some old cottages around the green, but is otherwise entirely modern in appearance. It derives its name from the de Burgh family. Only the foundations remain of Nork House, where the Buckle family lived from the fourteenth century until the 1930s.

When Preston Hawe, the modern residential estate west of the Brighton road was being built in 1952, one of the 'lost' villages of medieval England was uncovered by the bulldozers, giving 'the most complete picture of life in the Middle Ages so far discovered'. The reason for the disappearance of these 'lost villages' remains a mystery; it may have been due to the Black Death, the sudden drying up of the water supply, or the mere whim of a landowner, as at Cuddington.

Kingswood, with the soaring spire of the Victorian church of St Andrew's as a landmark for miles around, is south of Burgh Heath and higher on the Downs. There is no recorded mention of it before the fourteenth century. St Sophia's, or the Church of the Wisdom of God, in Lower Kingswood, was built in 1892, and is remarkable for its interior decoration, which includes Byzantine capitals brought

from Greece and Turkey, and elaborate woodwork. Two priests'
seats are inlaid with mother of pearl.

Kingswood Warren, a castellated Victorian mansion, is now used
as a research station for the BBC.

The Worthing road (A24) cuts through Ewell, where the springs
welling up in the centre of the village are the principal source of the
little Hogsmill River, and are said to be among the coldest in
England. Old Ewell is yet another Surrey village which has fought
against development plans, and saved its Tudor cottages, although
much had already disappeared.

Ewell makes the most of its little river, with its eighteenth-century
pack-horse bridge. Millais, who frequently stayed with the Lemprière
family at Ewell Manor in Cheam Road, found lodgings with his
friend, Holman Hunt, at Worcester Park Farm. Both used the
Hogsmill River as a background to some of their most famous
paintings.

Only the fifteenth-century tower remains of the old church, but
it has some attractive sixteenth-century brasses and eighteenth-
century monuments. James Lowe, who was buried in the churchyard, anticipated Sir Francis Pettit-Smith as an inventor of a
screw-propeller. After his death in 1866, his daughter, Henrietta
Vansittart, carried on with his experiments, and patented the
Lowe-Vansittart propeller, which was fitted to many Government
ships.

Another Ewell man was Richard Corbet, born in 1552, the son of
a gardener, who became famous as a poet and wit, and was successively Dean of Christ Church, Bishop of Oxford and Bishop of
Norwich.

On the east of Ewell is the finest of its many beautiful parks—
Nonsuch, once the hunting ground of Nonsuch Palace. The ancient
village of Cuddington was demolished by Henry VIII, and work was
begun on the palace in 1528, using stones from Merton Priory, and
bricks made locally. Intended to be so magnificent that there would
be 'nonsuch' in Christendom, the palace was much admired by
contemporaries, but as it was demolished little more than a century
later, it is difficult to be sure whether it was really as beautiful as
it was claimed to be. Overwhelmingly magnificent, perhaps, but

possibly vulgarly ostentatious, and certainly too expensive to maintain. Excavations carried out in 1959 revealed the whole of the ground plan, near Ewell by-pass.

John Evelyn says six lilacs were planted round the fountain. He described them as 'trees which bear no fruit, but only a most pleasant smell'. They are said to have been the first lilacs introduced into England.

Much of the stonework of Nonsuch Palace was used after its demolition to build houses in Epsom, then rising in popularity as the result of the discovery of the medicinal properties of Epsom Wells. It became very fashionable after the Restoration, and the institution of the Derby in 1780 by the twelfth Earl of Derby ensured the influx of ever-increasing crowds.

Even those least interested in racing cannot escape knowledge of the world-famous races on Epsom Downs during Derby Week, especially since radio and television gave it world-wide publicity, and there can be few who have not seen a reproduction of Frith's picture *Derby Day*, the original of which is in the Tate Gallery. It was at a gathering at the Earl of Derby's mansion 'The Oaks' (since demolished) that it was resolved to institute the races and name the principal events after the Duke and his house.

Quite apart from its races, Epsom has a long history. Relics from the Mesolithic period to the time of the Saxons have been dug up, showing the site was occupied from very early times, and documentary evidence begins in AD 675. Although the character of the High Street was entirely changed during road-widening, Epsom has many late Stuart, Queen Anne and Georgian buildings, particularly in Church Street, South Street and Woodcote. St Martin's Church was rebuilt in 1824, with the exception of the Perpendicular tower, but has seventeenth-century monuments, including one to Elizabeth Evelyn, who died in 1691. She was the first to obtain the right for a market and two fairs to be held in Epsom.

Epsom's many famous residents and visitors include such diverse characters as the scholarly Sharon Turner, an authority on Icelandic and Early Saxon languages; Mrs Beeton, of cookery-book fame, and the fifth Earl of Rosebery, who was Liberal Prime Minister 1894–6, and owner of the Derby winners of 1894, 1895 and 1905. He lived at

Durdans, an eighteenth-century house on the site of an earlier mansion, between Woodcote Road and Chalk Lane

Tadworth, south of Epsom, has a modern estate and a magnificent seventeenth-century house, Tadworth Court, now a branch of the famous Great Ormond Street Children's Hospital.

There is some of the grandest walking country in Surrey between Epsom Downs and Box Hill. Walton-on-the-Hill (to distinguish it from Walton-on-Thames) is probably best known for its golf course on Walton Heath. It has had a long succession of royal or noble owners, but most of its houses are Victorian. A Romano-British villa was excavated at Sandilands Road, north of Walton, in 1948–9.

St Peter's Church has been over-restored, but has some good Perpendicular work, and a leaden font dating from the twelfth century which is probably the oldest surviving lead font in England. It has been reduced in size at some time, but still has eight seated figures in high relief.

Headley, on a windswept, furzy plateau with splendid views, is threatened by the proposed line of the M25, planned to cross the Downs just south of the church, which is Victorian, with some eighteenth-century tablets in the vestry. Some of the stones of the old church have been built into a curious grotto in the churchyard. Emily Faithfull, who was born in the rectory in 1835, when her father was rector, established a printing press in London in which only women were employed, with the object of extending their then painfully limited sphere of labour. It soon gained a reputation for its excellent work, and she was appointed Printer and Publisher in Ordinary to Queen Victoria. She also published the *Victorian Magazine*, in which she strongly advocated the claims of women for remunerative employment.

Box Hill was already a popular 'diversion' for people from Epsom in Celia Fiennes' time, Defoe writes of an 'abundance of gentlemen and ladies from Epsom [who came] to take the air, and walk in the box-woods', and in Jane Austen's day it was the obvious choice for the excursion of Emma and her friends which ended so disastrously.

The beautiful wooded hill, which rises steeply on the east of the Mole valley, gives views across the 24 miles of the western Weald to the South Downs, dominated by Chanctonbury, which is almost due south of Box Hill. South-west is Dorking and wooded Leith Hill, easily recognized by its tower, and north-west there are far-reaching views from Juniper Top and Mickleham Downs across the valley of the Mole to the River Thames. Box Hill and its immediate neighbourhood is carefully preserved by the National Trust, which has gradually acquired most of the area through public and private generosity.

Immense crowds flock to the summit of Box Hill on fine summer week-ends, many of them especially intrigued by the stone where the eccentric Major Peter Labillière of Dorking was buried upside down, at his own request, so that 'as the world was turned topsy turvy, he might come right at last'. Even more people patronize the tea-room and ice-cream parlour. It is more rewarding for those fortunate enough to be able to choose their own time, to visit Box Hill on a week-day, preferably before or after the time for any coach trips.

The River Mole, which turns north near Box Hill Bridge to flow through the Mole Gap, has figured in the works of Spenser, Milton, Dryden and many others, all of whom emphasize its curious habit of disappearing underground at times. Celia Fiennes explains that 'just about Dorken and Leatherhead it sinkes away in many places which they call swallow holes'. The river still disappears from sight in dry seasons.

Roman Stane Street crossed the River Mole by a ford, discovered in 1937 when the by-pass and the new Burford Bridge were being constructed. A portion of the actual surface of the road was excavated in the grounds of Juniper Hall many years ago.

Contrary to a general belief, the much-photographed Stepping Stones are not old. They were originally put in position in 1932, but by 1946 had deteriorated so greatly that they were replaced at the expense of James Chuter Ede, then Home Secretary, who had spent his school days in the district, and had many links with Surrey. They were opened by Clement Attlee, then Prime Minister, who had family associations with the neighbourhood.

A short distance downstream is an iron footbridge built as a memorial to members of the Ramblers' Association who died in the two World Wars.

The villages and mansions of this most delightful valley have associations with many famous people. The Burford Bridge Hotel, where the Mickleham by-pass turns off from the old London to Worthing road, was formerly known as the Fox and Hounds. It has been extended and modernized until it would hardly be recognized by the celebrities who flocked there in the nineteenth century. Here Nelson stayed before the Battle of Trafalgar, and took his last farewell of Lady Hamilton; Keats wrote *Endymion*; Robert Louis Stevenson was a frequent visitor between 1878 and 1886, and wrote part of *The New Arabian Nights*.

On the other side of the river is the village of West Humble and the turreted Boxhill and Westhumble Station. Cleveland Lodge, the home of Lady Jeans, widow of Sir James Jeans, has a lovely garden and is a perfect setting for the annual Music Festival established by Susi Jeans and Stephen Manton in 1954 as the Mickleham and West Humble Festival. The name was changed to the Boxhill Music Festival in 1965, but it continues to concentrate on music of the sixteenth, seventeenth and eighteenth centuries.

Susi Jeans has specialized in playing the organ, harpsichord and clavichord, and her Music Room at Cleveland Lodge contains two clavichords, a pedal harpsichord and four organs, one of which was built to the specification of Sir James Jeans. Among well-known musicians who have taken part in the Festival are Thurston Dart, Leon Goossens, Julian Bream, Anthony Hopkins, Matyas Seiber, Alfred Deller, Marjorie Lavers and Christopher Monk. There is always an interesting programme, combining well-known works with items which have suffered undeserved neglect. The 1968 Festival was based on the happy idea of featuring music especially linked with Cleveland Lodge and its neighbourhood, which included works by Mendelssohn, an aunt of whom once owned Cleveland Lodge, and Stephen Storace, the eighteenth-century composer who studied under Mozart; Dr Charles Burney, the musicologist, whose daughter Fanny was married in Mickleham Church, and John Marsh, who was born at Dorking in 1752.

Also in West Humble is Camilla Lacey, a modern housing estate on the site of the house Fanny Burney built with the money she earned with her novel *Camilla*, in the garden of which her husband became an enthusiastic but highly unorthodox gardener. Farther north, on the old London road, is the village of Mickleham, the charm of which has been preserved through the construction of the by-pass. The Norman church has been much restored and is now chiefly known as the church in which Fanny Burney married General D'Arblay in 1793, and George Meredith married his second wife, Marie, daughter of James Vulliamy of the Old Hall, Mickleham, in 1864. The Merediths lived at Flint Cottage, on Box Hill, which became a place of pilgrimage for all the leading writers and young aspirants to fame, including Stevenson, Kipling, Barrie, Henry James and Wilfred Blunt. Leslie Stephen's Society of Sunday Tramps met there frequently to climb Box Hill or Leith Hill with Meredith, who was a dedicated walker and lover of nature. He died at Flint Cottage in 1909 and is buried in Dorking Cemetery, in sight of Box Hill.

Juniper Hall, where General D'Arblay lived with a group of such distinguished French émigrés as Mme de Staël, MM de Narbonne and Talleyrand, was bought in 1814 by Thomas Broadwood, a junior partner in the famous firm of piano-makers, and in 1945 by the National Trust. It is let to the Council for the Promotion of Field Studies.

West of the London road, and almost opposite Juniper Hall is Fredley Manor, where Richard 'Conversation' Sharp entertained innumerable literary and political celebrities in the early nineteenth century. Farther north, west of the river and by-pass, is Norbury Park, on a magnificent site giving fine views of the Mole Gap and its surrounding hills. The house dates from the eighteenth century and is famous for its 'painted room', with walls and ceiling painted with landscapes which blend with the views from the windows. It was while Fanny Burney was staying at Norbury Park with her friends the Lockes that she met her future husband. Norbury Park now belongs to the Surrey County Council, and much of the estate is open to the public, including the 'Druids Grove' with its venerable yew trees.

Leatherhead, at the north-west end of the Mole Gap, is reached from the A24 Mickleham by-pass by the quaintly named Gimcrack Hill, which merges into Church Street. The twelfth-century church of St Mary and St Nicholas is more clearly Norman inside than on the exterior. It has a few eighteenth-century monuments. Mrs Diana Turnor, great-granddaughter of Lord Burghley, Elizabeth I's Minister of State, was buried in the porch, at her own request, on the spot where her sedan chair stood when she attended services. Anthony Hope Hawkins, the creator of Ruritania, whose father, the Rev. E. C. Hawkins, was Headmaster of St John's Foundation School, is buried in the churchyard.

Among others who have lived in Leatherhead are Robert Gardyner, Elizabeth I's Chief Sergeant of the Cellar, who lived at Thorncroft; Richard Dalton, Sergeant of the Wine Cellars to Charles II; and Sir Thomas Bludworth, Lord Mayor of London in 1666, who lived at The Mansion. His daughter was the second wife of Judge Jeffreys. The Council Offices mark the site of Kingston House, where John Wesley preached for the last time, on 27 September 1791.

Leatherhead has been identified with Jane Austen's 'Highbury'. As E. V. Lucas points out in his Introduction to the World's Classics edition of *Emma* '. . . Leatherhead fulfils most of the conditions. It is rightly placed with regard to London, Kingston and Box Hill; it has a river, and I am told (but this may be pure coincidence) both an Abbey Farm and a Randalls!'

The opening of the Thorndike Theatre in Church Street in 1969 has done much to revitalize the community life of Leatherhead. The attached studio theatre is named the Casson after Dame Sybil Thorndike's husband, Sir Lewis Casson.

Several sixteenth-century buildings survive in Leatherhead, most of them much restored. Sweech House, in Gravel Hill, was presented in 1947 to the Leatherhead Country Protection Society.

The bridge across the Mole, with its 14 arches, was first built in 1782, and has been widened more than once. At the foot of Bridge Street is the timber-framed Runnynge Horse, which was kept in the sixteenth century by Eleanor Rumming or Romyng, who was the subject of *The Tunnyng* of Eleanor Rumming*, a libellous humorous poem, chiefly distinguished for its coarseness, by the Poet Laureate John Skelton, who is said to have visited Leatherhead frequently to

* *Brewing*

fish in the River Mole. The Leatherhead Historical Society has done a great deal of research on the subject, and has found Court Rolls recording that Eleanor Romyng was 'a common Tippler of ale and sells at excessive prices by small measures'—but in fairness it must be added that other local innkeepers were fined frequently for the same offences. Records of the Romyng family in Leatherhead go back to the late fourteenth century.

Ashstead, north of Leatherhead, is mentioned several times by Pepys, whose 'cozen' lived there. It developed greatly in the 1930s, but still has Ashstead Woods and Common, much favoured by ramblers. St Giles's Church, which dates from the Saxon period, has been much restored and rebuilt, but has some attractive monuments and sixteenth-century stained glass. The church is set in a triangular earthwork, with Roman material incorporated in it which is believed to have come from a Roman villa. It stands apart from the town, near Ashstead Park, which was rebuilt in the eighteenth century on the site of the house where Evelyn was 'entertained very civilly' by Sir Robert Howard, son of the first Earl of Berkshire, in 1684 'at his newbuilt house, which stands in a park on the Down . . .'.

West of Leatherhead, and north of the Guildford Road (A246), is Fetcham, now almost entirely joined up to Leatherhead. It is an attractive modern residential area, but dates back to Saxon times. A Saxon cemetery was found on Hawkes Hill during building developments, and there are traces of Saxon work in the rather dark church, which has grown through the centuries, and has been fortunate enough to escape over-restoration in the nineteenth century. Several of the memorials are worth more than a passing glance for their excellent carving. Among those buried in the churchyard are Admiral Sir George Henry Richardson, the hydrographer and promoter of submarine telegraphy, who as a young Commander went on an expedition in search of the ill-fated Arctic explorer, Sir John Franklin, and Sir Francis Graham Moon, printer and publisher, who became the acknowledged head of his profession, and was Lord Mayor of London in 1854. His eldest son, Sir Edward Graham Moon, was rector and patron of Fetcham from 1859 until his death in 1904.

Fetcham Park, the large red-brick house beside the church, was built by Arthur Moore, who is said to have started life as a footman. He studied trade questions, made money rapidly, became a very capable MP who 'knew everybody', and figured frequently in the poems, pamphlets and satires of his day, including those of Pope and Gay. He was buried at Fetcham in 1730.

By far the most interesting sight in Fetcham is an age-old natural phenomenon, now being put to practical use by the East Surrey Water Company. Eric Parker, who saw the springs in Fetcham mill pond in 1908, waxes lyrical over the strange and almost eerie effect of the constant movement of one part of the pond as springs quietly but persistently bubble up through the blue-green water, in contrast to the still, intense green of the rest of the mill-pond. The pond has been scheduled as a site of Special Scientific Interest, yet few of those who drive along the A246 suspect its existence. The Water Board, which acquired the site in 1957, reversed the usual process of flooding agricultural land for a reservoir. The pond, which had become silted up, was cleared, and the 'spring pits' were cut off by concrete walls. Now the quiet waters are a haunt of waterfowl, but the springs lie beneath a field, in which manholes have been left to enable them to be seen bubbling away several feet below the ground. The East Surrey Water Company, always anxious to make the public more water-conscious, encourages visits not only by hydrographers and geologists, but by organized parties of school-children, Women's Institutes and other groups. Three million gallons of water are taken daily from the springs, and another half million gallons a week to maintain the fresh water of the pond.

Between Fetcham and Guildford there is a series of 'paired' villages, of which the first, Great and Little Bookham, are now almost continuous with Fetcham. The Saxon church at Great Bookham was almost entirely rebuilt by the Normans. A chancel was added in 1341, and the Slyfield Chapel in the mid-fifteenth century. It has brasses and monuments to the Slyfields, Shiers, Howards and Moores, the earliest of which is dated 1433.

A monument to Cornet Geary, son of Admiral Geary of Polesden Lacy, who was killed in an ambush at Flemington, New Jersey, in 1776, shows British troops marching down a road, with American sharpshooters hiding in nearby woods. The most unusual, and most conspicuous monument commemorates the family of Gerrard Andrewes, Dean of Canterbury. The mural is half-hidden by an enormous carved weeping willow tree, with the leaves coloured a soft green.

The illustrated guide has a note on the many distinguished people who have worshipped in the church, including Jane Austen, whose godfather, the Rev. Samuel Cooke, was rector of Great Bookham from 1769 until his death in 1820; Fanny Burney, who lived at Fairfield (now The Hermitage) for the first four years of her married life, and whose son was baptized in the church, and the Duke and Duchess of York (afterwards George VI and Queen Elizabeth), when spending part of their honeymoon at Polesden Lacy.

The great house, which lies south of the Guildford Road, was given to the National Trust in 1942 by the noted society hostess, the Hon. Mrs Greville, and is open at advertised times. The illustrated guide gives many details of former owners, including Richard Brinsley Sheridan, who built the long terraced walk.

Little Bookham has a manor-house with a nineteenth-century front, owned for many generations by the Pollen family. Meredith White Townsend, proprietor and joint editor of *The Spectator* from 1860 to 1898, lived there from 1899 until his death in 1911, and is buried in the churchyard. The extremely attractive church is chiefly Norman. It is one of the ever-increasing number of churches which has to be kept locked. When I was there in 1974 the key was kept at Beer Cottage in Water Lane.

Effingham, from which the famous Howard family took its title, was granted to Lord William Howard at the Dissolution. It is now developing as a pleasant residential centre, and nothing of the past remains but a few cottages and farmhouses scattered over the large parish. *The History of Effingham* has been compiled by Monica M. O'Connor for the Effingham Women's Institute.

The village of East Horsley, including the church and mansion, was almost entirely rebuilt about 1860 by the eighth Lord King, who bought the manor in 1837, the year in which he was created Earl of Lovelace. He was an architect and civil engineer, and transformed the original pleasant mansion built by Sir Charles Barry in 1820 to his own design—and what a design! It has to be seen to be believed in its riot of flint and brick dressings and château-like towers, which it has been said 'would be a credit to the mad King Ludwig of Bavaria'. It is approached by 'the most sensational drive in England' —a long curved tunnel leading to a horse-shoe shaped cloister, beyond which is another short tunnel and archway, which is said to have been designed with a truly Victorian desire to keep the tradesmen out of sight of the noble owners and their guests! Today it is the only one of the original five carriage drives in general use, but as the tunnel is narrow and dark, no one is allowed to enter it on foot.

Apart from its monstrosity value, the house is of considerable interest for the use of the process of bending wood by steam, on which the Earl was an authority. The chapel, a riot of coloured glass windows, Minton tiles and carved stone and marble, has a plaque to his Countess, Ada Augusta, daughter of Lord Byron.

Horsley Towers was bought in 1939 by the Central Electricity Board, and is now a Residential Training Establishment of the Electricity Council.

East Horsley belonged to the Bishops of Exeter and among the brasses to the church is one of Bishop John (1478) of unusual design.

West Horsley Church is on a low knoll beside the main road, half way between East and West Horsley. Founded before the Norman Conquest, and chiefly of Norman and Tudor work, it has a shingled spire with louvre openings, some ancient glass medallions, a parish chest of about 1200, interesting brasses and one of the earliest stone effigies in Surrey of a priest, possibly Ralph de Berners, of 1377. One of the monuments to the Nicholas family is said to be the work of Grinling Gibbons, and there is a charming mural to John Kendal, who died in 1750, aged 23, by Nicholas Read, a pupil of Roubiliac, which incorporates a delicate relief of a rose tree with one fallen blossom.

Carew, son of Sir Walter Raleigh, inherited West Horsley Place in 1643, on the death of his uncle Sir Nicholas Throckmorton, but sold it in 1665 to Sir Edward Nicholas. It is said that the head of Sir Walter Raleigh, which had been embalmed and kept by his widow until her death, is buried in West Horsley church. West Horsley

Place has been altered several times since the fifteenth century, and now has an eighteenth-century front.

Hatchlands lies well back from the road, but clearly visible, between West Horsley and East Clandon. It was built by Admiral and Mrs Edward Boscawen, and has the distinction that the interior decorations are the earliest known work carried out by Robert Adam. The house was transferred to the National Trust by H. S. Goodhart-Rendell, who wrote the informative illustrated guide. It is open on Wednesday and Saturday afternoons from April to September.

The Norman church of East Clandon, down a side road, is attractive both within and without. It is the only church in Surrey dedicated to St Thomas of Canterbury. The most striking monument is to Stuart, Lord Rendell, designed by his grandson, H. S. Goodhart-Rendell, with an elaborately patterned plaster ceiling over it.

One of the early seventeenth-century vicars was Thomas Goffe, 'a quaint preacher and a person of excellent language and expression' who was a playwright and an orator. Although a woman-hater, he was inveigled into marrying the wife of his predecessor, but she and her daughters soon gave him cause to regret it, and he died shortly after.

The Clandon Downs rise on the south of West Clandon village, which straggles north along the A247 to Clandon Station.

Although the church of St Peter and St Paul has twice been restored it still has an atmosphere of age. The carved Onslow pew at the west end of the church is probably of seventeenth-century Italian work. There is a quaint carving on a wooden panel above the door of the south porch, depicting two animals, sometimes described as a reptile and dragon, but more probably a dog and dragon, which appear to be fighting. It is believed to refer to a more than usually vague local legend of a dragon which lived in Send Marsh and terrorized the villagers. It was killed by a deserter from the army, with the help of his dog, on condition the villagers would procure him a pardon, which they duly did—although when or how is not clear.

Clandon Park, built in the first half of the eighteenth century, has spacious rooms and much period furniture. It was presented to the

14 (opposite above) *The south front of Polesden Lacy*

15 (opposite below) *Sutton Place from the south-east*

National Trust in 1956. The house and garden are open to the public from April to October, on most afternoons of the week, but the park is still privately owned. The illustrated guide includes an account of the Onslow family by Pamela, Countess of Onslow, who brings them vividly to life. Two things only seem to have remained constant— their close association with the town of Guildford, and with Parliament. Three Onslows rose to be Speakers of the House of Commons, of whom Arthur Onslow was by far the most admirable.

Huge fields separate Clandon Park from the built-up area of Guildford, where the River Wey breaks through the Downs.

Merrow, now almost merged into Guildford, has a rebuilt church with a few late Norman and thirteenth-century details, and graves of several of the Onslow family in the churchyard. Opposite the church is the Horse and Groom, dating from 1615, but with little of the original building left.

The A25 turns off the Guildford road to skirt the north-east of Merrow Down to the famous beauty spot of Newlands Corner, and turns left at Albury to run along the southern face of the Downs to the Kentish border.

John St Loe Strachey, proprietor and editor of *The Spectator* from 1898 to 1925, in succession to Meredith W. Townsend, bought land at Newlands Corner and built the house which is now the Newlands Hotel, because it had 'the finest view in Surrey'. Near the hotel is the Merrow Down racecourse on which races were held every Whit Week from the seventeenth century to the middle of the nineteenth century. It was the training ground of Eclipse, which St Loe Strachey described as 'the swiftest, the most beautiful, the most perfect horse that the world has ever seen . . . the hero of the old saying "Eclipse first, and the rest no-where" '. Born on the day of the eclipse in 1764, Eclipse did not have a single blemish, and was never beaten. His blood is said to flow in the veins of every English racing thoroughbred.

The 'grassy track' on Merrow Down of the poem in Kipling's *Just So Stories* was the old Hoar or Harrow Way, which still crosses Merrow Down close by Newlands Corner.

16 (opposite) *Kew Gardens with Syon House in the background*

CHAPTER SIX

Between the Downs and the Weald

Limpsfield to Guildford via Reigate and Dorking

The A25, which crosses Surrey from the Kentish border to the out-skirts of Guildford, along the narrow belt of Greensand and Gault, is never far from the southern foot of the North Downs, and any of the quick succession of delightful towns and villages along the road can be made a starting or halting point for those who are exploring the Old Road on foot, or for the great stretch of the Weald which lies south of the road, and away over the Sussex border.

Limpsfield, the first of the Surrey villages on the A25, lies at right angles to the busy main road. It has a single main street, with an attractive mingling of houses of all periods from the fifteenth century to the present day, the finest of which is Detillens. Unlike most large houses, it is only separated from the High Street by a small courtyard. It is a perfect example of a typical Wealden or Hall house, built about 1450, which has been altered through the centuries, as changing times brought an ever greater emphasis on comfort, without altering the essential beauty of the structure. The process at Detillens began in the early sixteenth century, when a second floor was inserted in the great Hall to make an upper story. The courtyard was enclosed to make another room, and fireplaces with ingle-nooks, chimneys and panelling were inserted. In the seventeenth century the fine Jacobean staircase replaced the former means of access to the upper floor.

When Mr Detillen, from whom the house derives its name, settled there about 1700, he gave the house a Georgian front with the then newly fashionable sash-windows, to let in more light and air. It is believed he was a Huguenot refugee, and that he was responsible also for much of the interior carving, which includes fleur-de-lys in the designs. The early history of the house and its previous name are unknown, but it was originally considerably larger, and included the cottages now in Detillens Lane.

Unobtrusive modern comforts, and much beautiful period furniture have been added by the present owners, Mr and Mrs D. G. Nevill, and although it is obviously a well-loved family home, it is open to the public on several afternoons a week from May to September.

Limpsfield church, with its massive Norman tower, is one of only five churches in Surrey in which a small oven for baking Communion wafers survives in the chancel. There are monuments to the families of Stanhope, Gresham and Elphinstone, including one to Eugenia Stanhope, the unwelcome daughter-in-law of Lord Chesterfield, whose generosity to her and her children she betrayed by selling his *Letters to My Son* to a publisher after the Earl's death.

When the funeral of the thirteenth Lord Elphinstone took place in 1860, it must have created something of a sensation in the quiet village, as the procession included his Chinese servants in their native costume.

Even more spectacular was the funeral of Frederick Delius, when Sir Thomas Beecham made a funeral oration, by torchlight, in tribute to the composer whose works he had helped to make widely known. Delius, who died and was buried in 1934 at Grez-sur-Loing in France, was brought to Limpsfield for re-burial in 1935, largely through the insistence of Beatrice Harrison, the 'cellist, and her sister May. Delius's wife is buried in the same grave, and Beatrice Harrison was buried in an adjoining grave in 1965.

Among others buried in the churchyard are Florence Barclay, who was born at Limpsfield in 1862, when her father, the Rev. S. Charlsworth was Rector, and achieved phenomenal success with her novel, *The Rosary*; Sir John Arthur Thomson, Professor of Natural History at Aberdeen University from 1899 to 1930, who devoted himself to making science readable; Sir Laming Worthington-Evans, who was Secretary of War for 1921–2 and 1924–9; and Harriet Kennard, a local heroine who, when over 80 years of age, nursed the workers constructing the railway in the nineteenth century when cholera broke out among them, until she herself died of the disease.

Old Oxted, a mile west of Limpsfield, is now by-passed by the A25. The High Street has formed a cutting up the steep hill, and a number of the cottages have steps from the road up to the front door and all, old and new, make an extremely attractive picture. The Crown Inn and the Bell although restored date from the fifteenth century. Unfortunately, the large golden bell which jutted out over the road has disappeared, and enquiries made when I visited Oxted in 1974 failed to reveal when or why this well-known landmark was removed.

The old parish church and manor-house are on the northern border of New Oxted, nearly a mile from the old village. The manor was bought in 1587 by Charles Hoskins of London, and it was probably he who abandoned Oxted Court and settled at Barrow Green Court, which has associations with Grote, the historian of Greece, Jeremy Bentham and J. S. Mill.

The church has a squat Norman tower, but has been much altered as a result of damage by lightning in 1637 and 1719, and of restoration in the Victorian era. It has some rewarding inscriptions for the collector of epitaphs. St Mary's owned some beautiful church plate, but this was auctioned at Christie's in 1974. It realized nearly £8,000. A valuable chalice which had been bequeathed to the church by Catherine, only daughter of John Hoskins, who married the third Duke of Devonshire in 1718, was bought by her descendant, the present Duke who, with great generosity gave it back to St Mary's. It is sad that in our sacrilegious times it has to be kept in a bank vault, and not in the church where it belongs.

Blunt House, now an Old People's Home, was built by J. Oldrid Scott for himself, and an old barn has been converted into the Barn Theatre to serve the needs of the community.

Foyle Riding, south of the A25, was the family home of the Harrison family, where Delius sometimes visited them. Beatrice Harrison used to broadcast her famous 'nightingale duets' in the grounds. She organized coach parties of East End children to come down and hear the nightingales, and gave them high tea afterwards. The five Harrison sisters moved to several farms in the neighbourhood after the death of their parents, before settling finally at Hollesley Farm, Smallfield.

Godstone, partly on the A25 and partly on the A22 to Eastbourne, which is here on the line of the old Roman road, has managed to preserve its village green and pond unharmed. There are also some fine old inns. The White Hart, founded in the reign of Edward II, and restored in the reign of Elizabeth I, changed its name to The Clayton Arms in the time of Sir Robert Clayton—of whom we shall hear more at Blechingly—and has only recently reverted to its original name. It is said to have provided accommodation for the Czar of Russia and his entourage in 1815, when they attended a prize fight at Blindley Heath.

St Nicholas's Church is on twelfth-century foundations, but was almost entirely rebuilt by Sir Gilbert Scott. Among its brasses and memorials is a monument to Sir John and Dame Tomasin Evelyn, kinsfolk of the diarist. It was this Sir John who inherited the family monopoly in the manufacture of gunpowder, and established a factory at Godstone.

Oakhurst Court, in South Godstone, where Barbu Jonescu, the Roumanian millionaire, entertained Prince Carol and Elena Lupescu for a few momentous weeks in 1928, is now divided into flats.

In spite of the fact that its wide High Street is a part of the A25, Blechingly (or Bletchingley) remains a delightful place. The Norman castle was demolished in 1264, in the war between Henry III and Simon de Montfort, and was never rebuilt. Slight traces can be found in the grounds of Castle Hill, and only the gatehouse remains, at Palace Farm, to mark the site of the magnificent palace built by Edward Stafford, Duke of Buckingham, in 1517. Both he and his successor, Sir Nicholas Carey, were executed, and Blechingly was settled upon Anne of Cleves after her divorce. She bequeathed it to her steward, Sir Thomas Cawarden, who had been Keeper of the Revels to Henry VIII.

Blechingly was a market town for centuries, and returned two Members of Parliament from 1294, although there were never more than 150 voters, and by the 1830s there were ten or less—which naturally aroused Cobbett's ire against it as a 'vile, rotten borough'.

Elections were held at the White Hart Inn from 1733 until the borough was dissolved under the Reform Bill.

The White Hart is an imposing sixteenth-century building with an eighteenth-century stucco front. It faces the open square of half-timbered houses flanking the approach to the church, one of which is a Tudor house built by Nicholas Woolmer, who paid only twopence a year for the land on which it stands. This is recorded in the Court Rolls of 1522, one of the many documents relating to life in Blechingly in the sixteenth and seventeenth centuries, which are now in the Surrey Record Office. A selection of these has been published recently.

The noble parish church reflects the past importance of Blechingly. The spacious interior is dominated by the enormous monument to Sir Robert Clayton, signed by Richard Crutcher. It is his only known work. The long epitaph records that Sir Robert was the son of a Northamptonshire carpenter, who amassed a huge fortune as a scrivener, became Lord Mayor of London, foreclosed on the Evelyn property at Godstone in 1677, and on the Peterborough property in Blechingly, and so became the greatest local landowner, but lost his wife and son before his own death in 1707.

The oldest of the brasses may be that to Hugh Hextall, chaplain to the Duke of Buckingham, who became rector in 1451. The church is full of interesting details, the most unusual of which is the model of a sailing boat, given by the islanders of Tristan da Cunha, in appreciation of the hospitality of the people of Blechingly when they evacuated their island after the volcanic eruption. They lived at Pendrell Camp, in the north of the parish, from 1961 to 1962.

Blechingly church sets the keynote of the community spirit of the village by opening its doors to regular weekly services for Roman Catholics and Methodists, as well as Anglicans.

Nutfield church is on a hillside north of the A25. It was restored in the nineteenth century, but has some ancient fittings and Burne-Jones windows. South Nutfield has two huge nineteenth-century mansions—Nutfield Priory, now a school for deaf children, and Lytell Hall, in which the Brewing Industry Research Foundation has been housed since 1948. All aspects of brewing are studied there, in the search for the 'perfect' beer. It is the only organization of its kind in the world, and attracts many foreign visitors.

Nutfield is almost entirely an agricultural district, its other long-established industry being the extraction of Fuller's earth from the soil. First exploited in the Roman era, it is now used for a wide range of purposes, including refining oil, glazing porcelain and for toilet preparations. Deposits of Fuller's earth are comparatively rare, and the factory exports to all parts of the world.

The Redhill aerodrome, south of the village, was used by the RAF in 1937–8, for training and operational flying and after Dunkirk it was used extensively by fighter aircraft during the Battle of Britain.

Reigate, on the old Brighton Road, originated in a Saxon village called Cherchefelle or Churchfield, near the site of the present church, and grew to importance under the autocratic rule of the de Warennes, Earls of Surrey. The family died out in 1374 and their estates passed to the Earls of Arundel, later created Dukes of Norfolk. The manor subsequently passed through many hands, and in 1922 was given by Somers Somerset to the Corporation.

Reigate was a Parliamentary Borough, returning two members to Parliament from 1295 until 1832, earning many sour comments from Cobbett.

The mound and dry fosse which are all that remain of the Norman castle are within two minutes' walk of the High Street. It was taken by Louis, Dauphin of France, in 1216, and slighted by the Parliamentarians—which sums up its undistinguished history.

The parish church has a twelfth-century nave and a chancel dating from the fourteenth and fifteenth centuries. The upper floor of the old vestry has a library of nearly 2,000 volumes, chiefly on theological subjects, founded by Andrew Cranston, who was vicar in 1701.

The baroque monument to Richard Ladbroke is one of only two sculptures known to be by Joseph Rose the Elder. A Victorian inscription records the death of Admiral Lord Howard of Effingham, lord of the manor of Effingham, who led the English fleet to victory over the Spanish Armada. He is buried in the vault beneath.

Reigate Priory, founded in the early thirteenth century for Augustinian Canons, was granted to Lord William Howard of

Effingham, who defeated the Scots at the Battle of Flodden Field. He was the father of the Admiral. He built a Tudor house, of which there are considerable remains, although from the outside it looks entirely of late eighteenth-century date. The interior has a superb fireplace, of which the origin is disputed, and an outstandingly fine eighteenth-century staircase painted with classical scenes, attributed to Verrio. The north courtyard is closed on the west by iron gates dating from about 1710, which have been compared to the work of the Davies brothers of Wrexham—high praise indeed!

Reigate has two windmills—an early nineteenth-century tower-mill on Wray Common, and a post-mill dating from 1765 on Reigate Heath, which has been used as a chapel since 1880.

The old Town Hall, built in 1728 on the site of St Thomas's Chapel, was spared when the New Town Hall was completed in 1931.

The Vale of Holmesdale, in which Reigate is set, is traditionally the scene of a rout of the Danes, which gave rise to a boast preserved in a couplet quoted by Camden:

The Vale of Homesdall
Never Wonne ne never shall.

But this, to quote Defoe, 'is a peice (*sic*) of history which I leave as I find it'.

Holmesdale Natural History Club Museum, in Croydon Road, has an extensive collection of British birds, insects, plants, fossils, minerals and mammals, which can be visited by appointment. The Club celebrated its Centenary in 1957, and the Centenary Booklet, a copy of which was presented to me by Mr B. Buckland Flint, the Hon. Archaeological Secretary, when I had the pleasure of giving a talk there, makes it clear how much the collections owe to the expert knowledge and generosity of distinguished members of the Club.

Also in Croydon Road is Cranham Lodge, where Eleanour Sinclair Rohde lived nearly all her life. Her dominant interest from her girlhood was in the history of gardening, and the culture of herbs, and her books are a valuable addition to garden lore. Mr G. W. Bingham, Reigate's local historian, tells me that during the Second World War she not only cultivated vegetables in her large garden, but employed a number of assistants to cultivate a considerable area in Alders Road and on Reigate Hill. In later years she developed a mail-order supply of herb seeds and plants, which gained her customers from all over Great Britain. She died in 1960.

In a series of articles contributed to the *Surrey Mirror* in 1963, Mr Bingham gives details of Reigate's many literary associations. Chief among them are George Eliot, who worked on *Daniel Deronda* at The Cottage, Earlswood Common, and Harrison Ainsworth, whose last 12 novels were written in Reigate. He died there in 1882. Richard Monckton Milnes, afterwards Lord Houghton, was a Governor of Redhill Royal Philanthropic School, and the Somers Somersets entertained J. A. Spender, Hilaire Belloc, Max Beerbohm, E. F. Benson, Eddie Marsh, Sir Sidney Colvin, W. B. Yeats, General Ian Hamilton and other notable literary figures.

Reigate was, of course, the setting for 'the singular and complex problem' of *The Reigate Squires* by Conan Doyle.

Gatton Manor came to the Copleys of Leigh in Tudor times, and in 1451 they were granted the privilege of sending two members to Parliament, and at one time Sir Richard Copley himself was the only inhabitant of the borough entitled to vote! It is not surprising Cobbett called Gatton 'a very rascally spot of earth'. How he must have chuckled when the Reform Bill of 1832 was passed and Lord Monson, who had bought the manor with its votes for two members for £100,000, two years previously, found himself with only the land as a result of his expenditure.

Sir Jeremiah Colman, founder of the famous firm of mustard manufacturers, built the present house with its impressive portico. Sir Jeremiah, who was Chairman of the Royal Horticultural Society's Orchid Committee for 21 years, grew an immense variety of orchids from all parts of the world, and hybrids of his own raising. He died in 1942. The mansion is now a school.

Close to the house is the small parish church which was transformed by Lord Monson in 1834 with elaborate panelling, stained glass and carved stalls acquired on his tours abroad.

One of the descendants of Edmund Shaw, a rector of Gatton, gave a new chapel to Colorado College, USA, for which a stone from Gatton church was sent to build into the fabric.

Near the house and church, on a hill, is an open Doric temple, built in 1765. Nominations for the borough were solemnly held there, and it is still known as 'Gatton Town Hall'

The enormous park is private, but there are several public paths across it, and the Old Road crosses it on the north.

Redhill, on the east of Reigate, only sprang up with the coming of the railway to Brighton in 1841, and it is now the most populous part of the borough. It derives its name from the colour of its sandy soil.

Merstham, in the north-east of Reigate, is still little more than a thriving village with a long history. The restored thirteenth-century church has some old brasses.

The famous cul-de-sac, Quality Street, was part of the old road to Croydon until the present road was built in 1807. It is said to owe its present name to a joking reference to Barrie's play, in which Sir Seymour Hicks and his wife, Ellaline Terriss, were acting. They lived at The Old Forge House in this enchanting backwater.

The great LCC estate is on the other side of the railway, hidden behind trees, but the village has to face the prospect of a multi-level junction of the M25 and M23 on the east.

The road to Dorking (A25) runs north of Reigate Heath and through Buckland where the green stretches north, giving a view of the Downs. West of the green is a curious wooden barn with a small turret at the end, which gives it the appearance of a small church.

The quiet little village of Betchworth lies well south of the main road, in a bend of the River Mole. Betchworth House with its Georgian front is between the bridge and the church in its tree-shaded churchyard. There are traces of Saxon and Norman work in the church, a chest hollowed out of a single tree trunk, and a bust of Sir Benjamin Brodie, who died in 1862 at Broome Park. He was President of the Royal Society, and of the Royal College of Surgeons.

Betchworth Clump, a spur of the North Downs crowned with beech trees, is a noted view-point on the far north-west of the parish.

Opposite the church is the attractive little Dolphin Inn, and a lane to Leigh which passes close to the fifteenth-century half-timbered More Place; Wonham Manor, with a brick 'Gothick' front and a white cupola, which can be glimpsed in passing; and Wonham

Mill, a nineteenth-century water-mill partly rebuilt in 1957, which is still working, and is, frankly, ugly.

The slight remains of Betchworth Castle, which was built in the sixteenth century and was a castle in name only, are on the golf course between Brockham Green and Dorking.

Brockham Green also lies well south of the main road, in another bend of the River Mole. The wide village green still has its village pump and its trim rebuilt church, against the superb background of the North Downs. Cricket was played on the green for centuries, and many famous cricketers, including the great W. G. Grace, have not disdained to play there, but in recent years the increasing hazard to motorists, who park their cars to watch games in progress, has forced the team to move to a safer pitch. The last of the famous triennial fairs was held about 1960.

Dorking is reached soon after crossing Deepdene Bridge across the River Mole. Deepdene House, the magnificent mansion of the Dukes of Norfolk, the gardens of which were so much admired by Aubrey and John Evelyn, stood east of the by-pass which bears its name. It was demolished in 1969, and a housing estate covers the site.

The gracefully curved High Street of Dorking has a raised pavement on the south, and although it preserves very few relics of earlier days, it contrives to retain the friendly atmosphere which seems inseparable from a genuine old market town. Its charm is enhanced by its idyllic situation in the Mole Valley between Box Hill and Ranmore Common, both of which can be seen from the heart of the town.

The site has been inhabited from very early times. Iron-Age, Roman and Saxon remains have been found, and the great Roman Stane Street cuts across the town, passing through what is now the north-west angle of St Martin's churchyard.

Dorking was destroyed by marauding Danes in AD 851, but since then has been one of the fortunate places which have very little history, although it suffered severely in the plague of 1603.

What Dorking lacks in history, is compensated for by its reputation among gourmets of earlier generations. Celia Fiennes rode through 'Dorken' in 1698, 'where are the best trouts in that river which runns by Boxhill . . .'. Dorking still has an Angling Society, but there are few, if any, 'trouts' there now.

Defoe says 'Darking' market was the most famous of all markets in England for its poultry, 'the name of Darking capon being well-known among the poulterers in Leaden-hall Market, some of these capons are so large as they are little inferior to turkeys'. The origin of the once famous Dorking fowls is disputed. Some authorities believe they were introduced to England by the Romans, but having regard to the fact that they always seem to have been known as 'Dorking fowls', and cannot be mistaken for any other breed, owing to the peculiarity that they have five claws instead of the usual four, it would seem reasonable to believe they are native to Dorking. Certainly Dorking people have long been known as 'Dorking chicks', and natives proudly claim to be known as 'Five Clawed 'Uns'. The cock is featured in the crest of the town's armorial bearings. Mr Christopher Belyavin, who is now one of the leading breeders of Dorking fowls, tells me they became almost extinct, owing to the difficulty of breeding them. They are now bred chiefly for show purposes.

Dorking was also famous at one time for wine made from wild cherries. Evelyn told Aubrey it was an excellent wine 'little inferior to French claret'.

Another speciality was a way of making water-souchy, a delicious dish of various kinds of fish, which were delivered to Dorking direct from 'Brighthelmstone' and Worthing. A recipe from a cookery book of 1833 is given by J. L. André in the *Surrey Archaeological Collections*.

Perhaps in these days when interest in regional dishes is growing, some enterprising restaurateur will revive these Dorking specialities, and draw gourmets once again to the town?

The soaring spire of St Martin's, rebuilt in 1868, dominates the town. It is Woodyer's most important church, but has few memorials of interest. The fine old White Horse Hotel, with its long eighteenth-century façade backed by half-timbering, is the most conspicuous building in the High Street, and there are one or two smaller inns to be found, but there are few other individually arresting buildings.

The Dorking Halls at the eastern end of the High Street were built in 1931 as a centre for the Leith Hill Music Festival and other local events. The now famous Festival originated in 1904, when a group of music lovers decided to launch a choral competition to stimulate local choral singing and instrumental playing. Miss Margaret Vaughan Williams became Secretary, and the following year her brother, Dr Ralph Vaughan Williams, conducted the first concert in Dorking. Choirs came from a ten-mile radius to take part, and the Festival became so popular that the concerts were extended in 1922 to three days.

Dr Vaughan Williams, who lived for many years at White Gates, Dorking, composed several choral works especially for the Festival, notably the *Benedicite*, which had its first performance at the 1930 Festival.

The Leith Hill Festival is the practical outcome of Dr Vaughan Williams's convictions, expounded in his *National Music*, that 'if the roots of your art are firmly planted in your own soil, and that soil has anything to give you, you may still gain the whole world and not lose your own soul'.

Dr Vaughan Williams resigned as conductor in 1953, but continued his association with the Festival as President until his death in 1958.

Many famous literary figures made their home in Dorking and its immediate neighbourhood, especially around Box Hill and Leith Hill. Edward Brayley, who was born at Lambeth (then in Surrey) in 1802, lived at Rose Hill, Dorking, where he wrote his *Topographical History of Surrey*. It is invaluable to historians for his descriptions and engravings of a changing Surrey which was still mainly rural.

William Mullins, a shopkeeper of Dorking, sailed in the *Mayflower*, and the courtship of his daughter Priscilla by Miles Standish and John Alden is told by Longfellow.

Cricket has been played at Dorking on the Cotmandene, the open space behind St Martin's Church, since 1777, and probably earlier. It was on this ground that Henry Jupp, the Surrey County cricketer, and Caffyn, both natives of Dorking, learned the game. Caffyn emigrated to Australia and greatly influenced cricket there before his death in 1919. Jupp, and Tom Humphrey of Mitcham, kept pubs in Dorking.

The Leith Hill and Box Hill Music Festivals, and the wonderful scenery of Dorking's surroundings, draw many people to the town, but there is also a large number attracted by the fame of two men who never lived—the immortal Tony Weller and his son, Sam. Most of them are happy to accept the White Horse as the original of the 'Marquis of Granby', but Dickens himself, in an unsigned but characteristic article in *All the Year Round*, says he conceived the 'Markis' to be the King's Head, at the corner of High Street and South Street. The site is now occupied by a bank.

The A25 continues westward from Dorking, skirting the southern foot of Ranmore Common to Westcott, an attractive village around a green, which still has its stone-walled pound, and is overlooked by the little Victorian church. In Squire's Wood, south of Westcott, is Mag's Well, one of the sources of the Pipp Brook, a tributary of the River Mole.

Westcott is set where the chalk Downs and the sandstone Surrey Hills run more or less parallel within a few yards of one another, and in the two miles of tree-shaded road between Westcott and Wotton the watershed between the Mole and its tributaries, and the tributaries of the River Wey is passed. South of the road is The Rookery, bought in 1759 by Daniel Malthus, who is buried at Wotton. His son, T. R. Malthus, the economist, was born there in 1766. A block of luxury flats now occupies the site.

Wotton House, bought by George Evelyn, grandfather of the diarist, in 1579, is in the valley of the River Tillingbourne, described by Aubrey as 'a little romancy vale'. John Evelyn's dearly loved birthplace, and the gardens he laid out, are much altered, but he has a permanent memorial in the woods of Leith Hill and its surroundings, which he planted. He was a passionate advocate of the re-afforestation of the countryside after the Civil War, and we have him to thank for many of the avenues and woodlands which survive in England today. He was also the first of the great English landscape gardeners, and led the revolt against Tudor formalism.

Wotton House is now a Fire Service College, but an Evelyn descended from another branch of the same family is still lord of the manor and patron of the living, and has a house on the estate.

There is no village at Wotton, and the church is down a lane on the north of the A25. Owing to its isolation, and recent vandalism there, it has been found necessary to keep it locked. Visitors will save time by fetching the key beforehand from the rectory, behind the Wotton Hatch Hotel, at the junction of the A25 and a lane running south to Friday Street and Leith Hill.

The large and handsome church of Wotton has an early Norman tower and much thirteenth-century work. Small carved heads, about three inches in height, above the south door, have been tentatively identified as those of King John, Archbishop Stephen Langton, Pope Innocent III and others of the period, but these identifications have been disputed.

The chief attraction of the church is, of course, the Evelyn Chapel, entered under an oak arch dated 1634, which is almost the only example of woodwork of that period in a Surrey church. The splendid monuments give a pictorial history of this important Surrey family.

The churchyard commands a panoramic view of the North Downs. North-west of the church is the grave of Richard Glanville, nephew of John Evelyn, under whose will a ceremony has been held annually in February. Local boys, by reciting the Creed, the Lord's Prayer and the Ten Commandments, with a hand resting on the tomb, and afterwards reading and writing portions of 1 Corinthians, Chapter 15, receive £2. They receive a further £10 if willing to be apprenticed to a trade. This custom has unfortunately been in abeyance for the last few years, but it is hoped to resume it when some financial problems have been sorted out.

Between the A25 and the Tillingbourne River are Crossways Farm, one of the most perfect small Jacobean houses in Surrey, which it is said George Meredith used as the background of *Diana of the Crossways*, and fifteenth-century Paddington Farm, which has overhanging gables.

A large and well-kept village green, where cricket is still played, borders the road just before the clock of Abinger Hammer comes into sight, projecting over the main road, with 'Jack the Hammer' striking the hours on his bell. The clock was erected in memory of Thomas Farrer, first Lord Farrer of Abinger, who died in 1899 at Abinger Hall, which has since been demolished.

The name of the village is not derived from the clock, but distinguishes it from the village of Abinger, to the south-east. Abinger Hammer was one of the many villages in Surrey where iron was made even before the time of the Romans. It continued to be an important industry until the eighteenth century. The Old Forge at Abinger Hammer is said to date from the early sixteenth century.

North of Abinger Hammer are the Hackhurst Downs, on which a granite pillar marks the place where Samuel Wilberforce, Bishop of Winchester—son of William Wilberforce the Abolitionist—was thrown from his horse in 1873, and received fatal injuries.

There are hammer ponds planted with watercress for a mile and a half between Abinger Hammer and Shere.

At Gomshall the road is close beside a bend of the River Tillingbourne, and passes under the Reigate to Guildford railway line—one of the few places where it is possible to glimpse the line from the road. Gomshall is an attractive place, with a picturesque wooden mill beside a footbridge across the Tillingbourne. A leather goods factory, well-hidden from the main road, is the sole reminder of Gomshall's long tradition as a centre for leather work, which dates back at least to Norman times. Beyond Gomshall the road runs through woodlands to the Shere by-pass.

Shere is a beauty-spot of such long standing that its main street is crowded with sightseers on summer week-ends, and it makes rather more provision for visitors than most places in the area.

There was a church at Shere in Saxon times, and it is mentioned as 'Essira' in Domesday Book. St James's dates from the Norman period, with later additions all carefully restored between 1956 and 1966. It has the best example in the county of a font dating from 1200, an early thirteenth-century chest, some medieval stained glass and fifteenth-century brasses.

In the north wall of the chancel are a squint and quatrefoil, which are all that remain of the cell of an anchoress. The Egerton manuscripts in the British Museum tell of 'Christine, daughter of William called the Carpenter, of Schere', who asked permission from the

17 (opposite) *The Clayton monument, Blechingly Church*

Bishop of Winchester to be enclosed in a cell attached to the church at Shere. The Bishop gave his consent on 14 August 1329. Three years later, Christine apparently regretted her decision—which is not surprising when it is realized the tiny cell had been built so that no sunlight could reach it. The Bishop did not take kindly to her defection, and issued a document saying 'now forswearing this life and conduct that she assumed, she has left inconstantly and returned to the world'. Finally, he allowed (or compelled?) her to return, with the proviso that she was to be guarded 'with suitable solicitude and competent vigilance' to ensure that 'the said Christine shall not wander from the laudable intention otherwise solemnly undertaken and again run about being torn to pieces by the attacks of the Tempter'. It is tantalizing that there is nothing to show how the affair ended.

Shere had a Barn Theatre in the 1930s where Peter Ustinov made his first appearance on the stage in 1938 with the Otherwise Players.

The Post Office and Bodryn, in the High Street, date from about 1600, and the White Hart Hotel, facing the church across the square, although refronted, dates back to the sixteenth century.

The manor of Shere was granted to Sir Reginald de Bray, who was high in the favour of Henry VII. Sir Reginald built the Bray Chapel in St George's, Windsor Castle, at his own expense, and is said to have been the designer of the Henry VII chapel in Westminster Abbey.

Another prominent member of the family was William Bray, who was born in 1736. In 1801, on the death of the Rev. Owen Manning, who had begun a history of Surrey, Bray undertook to complete the work, and visited every church and parish in the county. It is still considered one of the best county histories in England. Bray died in 1832, at the age of 96, and there is a mural to him in the church.

J. M. Barrie borrowed Anchor Cottage, Shere, from William Robertson Nicholl, editor of *The British Weekly*, in 1891, and wrote *The Professor's Love Story* there.

There is a far-reaching view south over the Surrey Hills on leaving Shere by-pass, and a mile farther on there is a choice of roads to Guildford. The A25 turns north-west to join the A246, and the A248 runs south-west through Albury and Chilworth to the Shalford Road.

18 (opposite) *An arcade in The Borough, Farnham*

Immediately north of the fork is the Silent Pool, another noted Surrey beauty spot. There are actually two pools, in a thick wood of beech, holly and other trees. The Silent Pool is associated with the legend invented by Martin Tupper in his completely unhistorical novel, *Stephen Langton*. Tennyson, who particularly admired the pool, describes 'the splendour and ripply play of light on the stream as it gushed down from the chalk over the greensand bottom, the mackerel colours which flit about in the sunshine, and the network of the current on the surface of the pool like crystal smoke'.

Conspicuous above the A248 into Albury is the Apostolic Church built for the Irvingite sect in 1840 by Henry Drummond of Albury Park. Drummond, who bought Albury Park in 1819, has been much criticized for pulling down the old village and moving the inhabitants to a new village outside the park, but he was only completing a process begun in 1784 by Captain William Finch, who obtained magistrates' orders to close or re-route roads. Drummond employed Pugin to build the new village with its fantastic chimneys, which are its chief claim to fame.

John Evelyn laid out the gardens of the original Tudor manor-house. He says on 23 September 1670: 'To Albury, to see how that garden proceeded, which I found exactly done to the design and plot I had made.' The house was rebuilt by Pugin and has some magnificent fireplaces. An Adam fireplace was brought from Syon House, and an overmantel probably brought by Drummond from Holyrood House. Much of Evelyn's garden design remains, including the terraces and a tunnel through the hill. Albury Park now belongs to the Mutual Household Association, and is open to the public on Wednesday and Thursday afternoons from May to September.

Martin Tupper entertained many notable visitors to Albury Park between 1850 and 1860, including Nathaniel Hawthorne, who ill repaid him with some unkind remarks in his *English Note-Books*. Tupper is forgotten now except as a synonym for the commonplace in verse, but he was an early friend to the colonizing of Liberia, encouraged African literature, was an ingenious inventor and a Fellow of the Royal Society. He died at Albury Park in 1889, and is buried in Albury churchyard. The finds he made when excavating on Farley Heath, on the site of one of the largest Romano-British settlements in the county, are in the British Museum.

The old church in the park, near the house, has been disused since 1842. The north wall of the nave and the base of the tower are believed to be Saxon, and the remainder is chiefly Norman or thirteenth-century work. The chancel is roofless, but the south transept was restored in the nineteenth century with brilliant wall decorations and stained glass. There are some early brasses and seventeenth- and eighteenth-century memorials.

William Oughtred, Rector of Albury from 1610 until his death in 1660, was one of the greatest mathematicians of his day, and is credited with inventing trigonometrical abbreviations. He died at Albury at the age of 85, and is said to be buried in the chancel.

The present parish church in Weston Street was built in 1842, and 16 years later Canon George Raymond Portal, a nephew of Henry Drummond, became rector. He was at Oxford with Thomas Hughes, author of *Tom Brown's Schooldays*, and the Rev. C. L. Dodgson (Lewis Carroll), who remained his life-long friends. Lewis Carroll frequently walked over from Guildford, and described the Old Rectory in his diary on 4 August 1888, as a '. . . very charming house, in a very pretty garden, and mine host and hostess are very pleasant and hospitable'.

It was in the library of the Old Rectory that Canon Portal and three friends founded the National Deposit Friendly Society. I have before me a copy of *The First Hundred Years, 1868–1968, The Story of the National Deposit Friendly Society*, by D. A. Roper and John Harrison, given to me by my old friend Robert Taylor, who was Chairman from 1959 until his death in 1972. It traces the Society's growth from its very small beginnings as a purely local society to its Centenary, when it had a capital of £27 million, and had achieved national importance.

Chilworth is the only village in the lovely valley of the Tillingbourne which has lost its simple charm in a rash of buildings. It was the chief industrial centre of the district, from the sixteenth century, when powder-mills were built there by George Evelyn, grandfather of the diarist, until the end of the First World War. Banknotes were also manufactured there, to the intense disgust of Cobbett, who thought gun-powder and bank-notes 'two of the most damnable inventions men had ever conceived . . . under the influence of the devil'.

Chilworth is sheltered on the north by the hill crowned by the isolated St Martha's Chapel, beside the Old Road, which was rebuilt in 1845 on its Norman foundations, using the original materials to impressive effect.

Chilworth Manor, dating from the seventeenth century, has a garden laid out on the site of an eleventh-century monastery. The walled garden is open to the public at advertised times.

The Tillingbourne joins the River Wey at Shalford, yet another of the lovely villages, full of character, in the 12-mile river valley.

CHAPTER SEVEN

The Weald

The Weald lies between the North Downs and the South Downs in Sussex, and spreads over into Kent on the east and Hampshire on the west. As Gertrude Jekyll, who lived in West Surrey, says: 'One steps without knowing it from Surrey into Hampshire and out of Surrey into Sussex, from one clay puddle into the next without being aware in either case, that the land is called by another name.' The same comment is true of East Surrey and Kent.

There are still large areas of woodland surviving from the days when the great forest of the Andredsweald, which the Romans called Anderida, was so dense that it was almost impenetrable. Even when Domesday Book was compiled, there was little to record, and it remained sparsely inhabited for centuries after the Norman Conquest. Its place-names are seldom those of early people or tribes, but refer to natural features, as in the case of Churt or Chart (a rough common, overgrown with gorse, broom and bracken); leigh or ley (a woodland or clearing); fold (a pasture) or hurst (a wood). When anyone did settle there in earlier times, it was usually to exploit the iron deposits, using the timber to build their houses, and to fire their furnaces for charcoal. When farmers made a clearing, they did not work in communal fields on the 'strip' system, but as individual settlers. Even today, the villages of the Weald are few and far between, reached by lanes which wind with seeming aimlessness, caused by the need to avoid some long-forgotten natural obstacle.

The Weald is still largely given over to agriculture, in spite of the difficulty of working the Wealden clay, and it is still true, as Cobbett observed, that three things grow well there—grass, wheat and oak trees.

Each of the towns and villages along the A25 can be made the starting point for exploring some part of the Weald.

The B269 runs south-east from Limpsfield over Limpsfield Common, with its woods and heathland, to The Chart, where it crosses the county border into Kent. The High Chart is a breezy hilltop common which has some genuine Wealden stone houses with brick dressings and steep-pitched tiled roofs.

Between Oxted and Godstone, a road turns south to Tandridge, which now gives its name to the whole new administrative area formed in April 1974—a reversion to its earlier importance. A plaque about 400 yards west of the Tandridge crossroads on the A25 says: 'On this hill, the Hundred's Knoll (known later as Undersnow) the Saxon Tythingmen from the surrounding villages of the Hundred of Tandridge met as the first local Government and Court in the Godstone Rural District.'

Tandridge church stands apart from the village surrounded by great trees, and is said to be on a site of pre-Christian worship. The huge yew tree in the churchyard is claimed to be so old that when the Saxon church was built its foundations were arched over the roots to avoid cutting them. The present church has some Norman work, and the shingled spire of the tower, which dates from about 1300, is one of the earliest of its kind in Surrey. It is supported internally by four oak posts of the same date which are each $14\frac{1}{2}$ inches square. The church was restored by Sir G. G. Scott, who lived at Rook's Nest, a Georgian house which is now Streete Court School. His wife is buried in the churchyard. Also in the churchyard are the graves of several members of the Pepys family, who lived at Tandridge Court, including Sir Charles Pepys, first Earl of Cottenham (1701–1851), who was twice Lord Chancellor of England.

The only remains of the Priory of Augustinian Canons, which was an off-shoot of Southwark, are the fish-ponds, north of the A25. It was never wealthy, and its record seems to have been a tarnished one. In 1308, the Cellarer was dismissed for falsifying the books, and more than one of the Priors was reprimanded for slackness.

Crowhurst church, south-east of Tandridge, has numerous memorials to the Gainsford or Gaynesford family, who acquired land at Crowhurst in the reign of Edward III, and of the Angells, who acquired Crowhurst Place in the sixteenth century. The fifteenth-century brasses show unusual details in the armour, but the memorial which attracts most attention is the only tombstone of Surrey iron in the county, duplicate castings of which were used as firebacks in many Surrey houses, and as far away as Norfolk. It is in memory of Anne Forster, daughter and heiress of Thomas Gainsford, who died in 1591.

The enormous churchyard yew is very ancient, but as an enterprising nineteenth-century innkeeper hollowed out the trunk, and fitted it with a door and a circular seat, it is not surprising that some of the branches show signs of decay. Efforts are now being made to save the remainder of its spread of living green.

Crowhurst Place, originally a wealthy yeoman's moated house built about 1425, was altered out of all recognition some time after 1918 in a fantasy of Tudor work.

Lingfield, directly south of Crowhurst, has been acclaimed in the past as the prettiest village in Surrey, and the grouping of half-timbered houses around the church is still perfection. The village pond and green at Plaistow Street, half a mile away, have deteriorated sadly. The green has been cemented and laid out with paths and flower beds. 'The Cage', beside the pond, which was built in the eighteenth century as a lock-up, is in disrepair, and modern houses crowd close.

Lingfield church is full of splendid monuments. But all the other brasses are outshone by the magnificent effigies of the Cobham family.

The first Lord Cobham fought at Crécy and grew rich on ransoms. His effigy is brightly coloured, with his head resting on his helmet, which has a Saracen's head as its crest, and his feet on a comical figure of a turbaned Saracen.

The brass to the second Lord Cobham, who supported Henry Bolingbroke, afterwards Henry IV, says he was 'brave as a leopard, sumptuous in his housekeeping, handsome, affable, magnificent and generous'.

The third Lord Cobham rebuilt the church, with the exception of the tower. He fought at Agincourt and died in 1446. Twenty-five years later, the family died out. His altar tomb has his effigy with that of his second wife, in alabaster.

The Cobham effigies, after surviving all the religious and civil disturbances of centuries, were damaged by vandals in our own degenerate days—on Good Friday, of all days!

Among innumerable other brasses, monuments, inscriptions and relics are two chained seventeenth-century books, and a chalice of 1572.

Close to the church is a Georgian house built of materials taken from the College founded on the same site in 1432 by the third Lord Cobham, of which nothing remains but the Guest House, now the Public Library. It was beautifully restored by C. Forster Hayward in 1898, and bequeathed to the Surrey County Council by his son in 1954, with a Trust fund for its maintenance. The original Hall is open to the roof, and has a gallery. The Children's Library was originally the buttery and kitchen, and the mechanical spit, operated by a rope and weight, is one of only three surviving in Surrey. There is a charming garden, which is also open to the public.

Five of the priests of the College are commemorated in the church by fifteenth-century brasses, and an inventory of the College's farm implements and livestock, made at the Dissolution, survives.

Almost opposite Lingfield Station is New Place, built in 1617 on an older site. It was standing empty in 1974. South of the village is the pretty Lingfield Park Race Course, which was constructed for National Hunt meetings in 1890, and extended for flat races four years later. It is passed on the way to Dormansland, a cluster of cottages on the outskirts of the park in which Greathed Manor stands. Formerly called Ford Manor, it was built in 1868 by Robert Ker, author of *The Gentleman's House*. It is now occupied by the Mutual Households Association Ltd, and the house and its beautiful garden are open to the public on Wednesday and Thursday afternoons from May to September.

North of Dormansland, on the Kentish border, is Starborough Castle. Built in 1342 by the first Lord Cobham, it was garrisoned for Parliament in the Civil War, and dismantled in 1649. Only the moat now remains, with a battlemented Gothic summer house built in 1754.

Still farther north, on the Lingfield Road to Edenbridge in Kent, is Puttenden Manor, the oldest portion of which was built in 1477

by Reginald Sondes, ancestor of Lord Sondes. The central portion
was repaired by Lord Rockingham in 1647 out of the ruins of the
original thirteenth-century manor-house, and a smaller wing was
added in 1905 by the Hon. Mark Napier, son of the tenth Lord
Napier. Among his many distinguished visitors were Sir Winston
Churchill, Lord Oxford and Asquith, Lord Reith and Hilaire Belloc.

Puttenden was restored in 1966 and is filled with fine furniture,
pictures and other relics. A remarkable exhibition of dolls made and
dressed in period costume by Mrs Mary Thompson, mother of the
present owner, is grouped against various appropriate backgrounds.
Especially amusing are the Edwardian 'parlour' and seaside scenes.
The house is open three afternoons a week during the summer.

South-west of Lingfield, at New Chapel, is a Mormon Temple,
with cool clean lines very different from the Weald vernacular, but
eminently pleasing. It is close to the junction of the Lingfield Road
(B2028) and the A22 to Felbridge on the Sussex border.

Farther west is Burstow, where there is no village, only a collection
of modern houses at the crossroads and several outlying hamlets.
A group of older houses around the church, deep among trees, keep
their seclusion, although their peace is shattered constantly by the
scream of aircraft from the airport at Gatwick.

The church of St Bartholomew was first mentioned in 1121, when
it was granted by Ralph, Archbishop of Canterbury, to the Cluniac
Priory of Lewes. It was probably reclaimed by the Archbishops in the
thirteenth century. The living ceased to be a peculiar of the See of
Canterbury in 1851, when it was united to Winchester. In 1878 it
was joined to Rochester, and is now in the diocese of Southwark.

The church has several features of interest, the most notable of
which is the fifteenth-century tower, one of the best in the county,
the only other comparable being at Newdigate. The remainder of
the church is chiefly Perpendicular with some Norman work. It has
a magnificent peal of bells, including one originally cast in 1450, and
the ringing chamber is level with and open to the nave. It has massive
supporting posts and beams.

John Flamsteed, the first Astronomer Royal, was Rector of
Burstow from 1684 until his death in 1719, and used the income from
the living to supplement his very meagre salary as Astronomer. He

paid only occasional visits to his curates at Burstow, but many of the letters he wrote to them give interesting sidelights on the affairs of the parish. They are preserved in the Observatory in Hurstmonceux Castle, and some are quoted by the Rev. C. A. Bingley, Rector of Burstow from 1950 until 1962, in *Some Aspects of Life in Old Burstow.*

Flamsteed is said to be buried in the chancel of the church but, although money for his monument was left in the will of his devoted wife, no monument has ever marked his grave. In more recent years, a stained-glass window was dedicated to his memory.

Close to the church are the sixteenth-century rectory, with additions made by Flamsteed and later rectors, and Burstow Court Lodge, now known as Old Court, on one of the four moated sites in the parish.

Only the moat remains of Rede, or Red Hall, but Burstow Lodge Farm, which was held by Roger Salaman in 1329, has been restored recently.

Moated Smallfield Place, a mile north of Burstow church, was built by John de Burstow on land given to him for personal service to Lord Burghersh in the French Wars. It was then called 'Crullings', but the name was changed to Smallfield as a condition of the gift. It was bought in 1613 by Edward Bysshe, a lawyer, who said the rebuilding he undertook was paid for with 'woodcocks' heads'—a cynical reference to the folly of his clients. He was succeeded by his son, Sir Edward Bysshe, who completed the house. He was Garter King of Arms in the Civil War period, and exerted himself to preserve the library of the College of Arms. Aubrey says he was 'active in iniquity of the times, ate the bread of loyalists and accepted a pension of £600 per annum from sequestrators'. Less prejudiced modern writers have praised his knowledge of heraldry. He died in London in 1679.

North of Smallfield are the wide common and beautiful woods of Outwood, a scattered hamlet which has a delightful cricket ground, and is dominated by a reconditioned post-mill, built in 1665. The neighbouring smock-mill, built about 1870, collapsed in 1960.

In spite of the proximity of the proposed route of the M23, there is hope this lovely region will be preserved, through the gifts made to the National Trust by Mr and Mrs T. H. Lloyd, totalling over

2,000 acres of farms, woods and cottages, including Burstow Park. Some parts of the old building remain, and it is administered as a farm by the National Trust.

A road runs directly north from Outwood through woodlands to the A25 at Blechingly.

Between the A23 from Reigate to Crawley and Brighton and the A24 from Dorking to Chichester there is a maze of roads south of the A25 to the sparsely scattered Wealden villages. Leigh (pronounced 'Lye') is one of the ironworking villages, which had to be sited on ore-bearing soil, where there were also good stretches of forest for charcoal burning. It is on a little tributary of the Mole. Leigh Place, an enchanting little *cottage ornée*, on a moated site plainly visible from the road, is passed before reaching the triangular green, which still has its well. The weatherboarded Plough Inn, on the north side, remains a delightful village inn, and there is a medieval Priest's House on the south-east.

The small Perpendicular church had a severe Victorian restoration, but has a brass to John Arderne, who died in 1449, with his wife and children. He was High Sheriff of Surrey, and lived in the original Leigh Place. There is a local tradition that Ben Jonson lived for a time in the late sixteenth-century house south-east of the village, now Swain's Farm, and much altered. There are several timbered cottages and farms in the parish, where agriculture is now almost the only industry.

The Six Bells Inn and old cottages of Newdigate are well away from the more modern houses, and close to the extremely attractive little church, with its many different styles of building. The oldest part is the Norman chancel, which was probably just a little chapel in the great Wealden forest. The interior of the massive medieval tower, with its supporting beams, resembles that at Burstow, which is the only other example of a timber tower in Surrey retaining its original plan. Here, again, the bell-ringers stand in full view of the people in the nave irreverent enough to turn their heads to see them. The excellent guide by Joyce Banks has pictures of the interior and exterior of the church at various stages of its existence, and descriptions of its monuments.

The de la Poyles, who built the Cudworth Chapel in the early fourteenth century to serve as a chantry or family chapel, lived at the neighbouring manor-house of Cudworth from at least 1298. Cudworth is chiefly fields and woods, with a farm, barn and manor-house only, the latter surrounded by a moat.

During the period when this book was being written, Charlwood, Horley and Gatwick were wrested from Surrey, to become part of the county of Sussex, but Horley and Charlwood fought a deter-mined campaign to remain in Surrey. A new boundary line has been submitted which it is hoped will be included in a new Parliamentary Bill allowing them to be returned to Surrey.

Charlwood, south-east of Newdigate, is another village which was once a centre for ironworks, but is now purely agricultural. The large and handsome church is chiefly fifteenth century, but with some Norman and thirteenth-century details, a fine late Perpendicular screen, and some notable wall-paintings discovered there in 1858.

There are attractive old cottages in the village, isolated medieval and Tudor farms, and traces of the 'causies' or causeways built to ensure ease of movement on the heavy clay soil in winter months. The history of Charlwood is told in the *The Free Men of Charlwood*, by Ruth Sewill and Elizabeth Lane.

The Sander or Sanders family, who first settled in Surrey at Sanderstead in the reign of King John, were at Charlwood Place from the reign of Edward II. Nicholas Sander, the Roman Catholic controversialist and historian, one of the 12 children of William Sander, was born at Charlwood Place about 1530.

Although Charlwood is close to the western border of Gatwick Airport, it has retained its identity as a village, but Horley, with the disadvantages of being astride both the A23 road and the main rail-way line to Brighton, and close to Gatwick Airport, has been swam-ped by modern developments. Its ancient church has been almost entirely rebuilt, apart from the fourteenth-century north arcade and doorway. It has two brasses, a late fourteenth-century figure of a civilian, a nearly life-size female figure of 1400, and a monument of a Salaman in early fourteenth-century armour with the double-headed eagle of the Salamans on his shield.

Next to the church is the Olde Six Bells, which really is old, although somewhat refurbished.

A moat a mile east of Horley beside the River Mole is all that remains of Thunderfield Castle, dating back to the time of King Alfred, in whose will it was mentioned as Dunresfield Castle. It has no other known history. As it is very close to the proposed line of the M23, it is hoped the Department of the Environment, in whose care it now is, will be able to save it from destruction.

Quite the loveliest of the Weald scenery lies west of the Dorking to Worthing Road (A24). Three Wealden villages lie on the road itself—North and South Holmwood, and Capel.

North Holmwood has suffered from its proximity to Dorking, and has been overwhelmed by development, yet immediately south is Holmwood Common, now in the care of the National Trust, spread out over 630 acres of open commons and woodlands to Holmwood Station. Beside the main road between North and South Holmwood is the granite memorial to Alfred Vanderbilt, the American millionaire who gave his life-belt to save an elderly woman from sinking in the *Lusitania*, although himself unable to swim. He was a devotee of coaching, and had a particular affection for this stretch of the Brighton Road.

The old Roman Stane Street ran west of the modern road, and the Surrey Archaeological Society has uncovered and restored a hundred feet of the Roman surface, which can be seen in Redlands Wood.

St Mary Magdalen, South Holmwood, dates chiefly from the mid-nineteenth century, and has a mural to George Rennie, son of the famous bridge builder, who entered into partnership with his younger brother after the death of their father in 1821, and completed the vast engineering works he had originated. George Rennie died in 1866 and is buried at South Holmwood.

St John the Baptist Church, Capel, was first mentioned in the eleventh century, and was originally known as the church of Ewekene, a name which survives in the farm of that name (spelled on the Ordnance maps as Eutons!). Eventually Capel (or chapel) superseded the name of the place which the chapel had been built to serve. The interesting history is given in a leaflet in the church, which details the Parliamentary Committee's disapproval of John Allen, curate of Capel who among other offences, had written a charm against toothache.

The present church dates mainly from the thirteenth century, with later alterations and enlargements. It has a shingled spire, and there is a monument to John Cooper dated 1590, on which he is kneeling in a red robe opposite his wife who is clad all in white. A staircase to the bell tower is a curious wooden version of a circular iron staircase.

There are a number of old houses and farms in the parish, and Temple Elfland has some Tudor work. It takes its name from the Knights Templars, who are supposed to have built the original house on the site.

Ockley is reached by a wooded road passing Ockley and Capel Station, Ockley church and Ockley Court. St Margaret's was almost rebuilt in 1873. There is a mosaic dado, but the interior is cold and uninviting, even on a hot day. The exterior, with a tower rebuilt in 1699, is more attractive. There is a stone mounting block by the entrance to the churchyard. The large eighteenth-century brick mansion is undistinguished architecturally. I must confess it is more memorable to me for the punnets of magnificent strawberries on sale there!

Both church and mansion are half a mile from the village, which is on a long straight stretch of the A29, here following the line of Roman Stane Street, and passing east of the beautiful, irregularly shaped village green. The green has an inviting seat under a little red roof, and some pleasant houses on the farther side, although the once attractive old Brewers' Arms has been modernized into the Old School House Restaurant. Leith Hill and the Downs make a superb background for the village cricketers.

Ockley Parish account books have been transcribed for the Surrey Archaeological Collections by Alfred Bax, and give a fascinating insight into the life of the village. There was a Post Office there at least as early as 1722. A curious entry in 1719 records: 'Mr Smith for lying Dead in his house, 1s.', without explaining why he (or, presumably, his heirs) should be paid for lying dead.

South of Ockley Green a rather unpromising turning on the south-west winds through shady woods of oak, beech and hazel to a tiny clearing in which the enchanting Okewood (or Oakwood) Chapel stands, on a little hill just large enough to take it with its small and beautifully kept churchyard. Wooden seats invite the visitor to sit in the sunshine and enjoy the utter tranquillity, which is almost unbelievable when it is remembered how close it is to the busy main road.

An excellent little *Handbook for Pilgrims* tells the story of how this little place of worship survived against many odds, entirely through the determination of its few and scattered parishioners.

Reputedly on the site of a Roman villa, which itself was on the site of a Druid temple, it was built about 1220, and restored and slightly enlarged in 1431 by Edward de la Hale. Legend tells that when he and his son were hunting wild boar in the forest surrounding the chapel, the boy fell from his horse in the path of a wounded boar, but an arrow whizzed through the air, killed the boar and saved the boy's life. In gratitude, de la Hale restored the building and endowed it with lands.

John Evelyn's *Diary* records on 14 July 1701 that he subscribed to another restoration of the chapel, but little seems to have been done, and it was not until the nineteenth century that another Evelyn of Wotton undertook the work of restoration. The floor of the nave was raised so much that the beautiful little brass to Edward de la Hale is six inches below the present level. When I was there in 1974 it was covered by a mat and a piece of boarding which had to be lifted before it could be seen, but there is a good reproduction of a rubbing, at the west entrance to the church.

Returning to Ockley, and turning north-east along the A29, the B2126 turns off on the left to Leith Hill, but it is well worth continuing to the next turning on the left, to Coldharbour. As the road climbs up through the woods to Coldharbour—one of several places which claim to be 'the highest village in Surrey'—there are glimpses now and again of a fine panoramic view of the North Downs. Just before reaching the village, there is a narrow turning on the right which passes several pleasant houses, among which is Kitlands.

The house was acquired in 1624 by the Bax family, who owned considerable property in the area, and became an important centre for the meetings of the Society of Friends. Thomas Bax of Kitlands was a direct ancestor of Sir Arnold Bax and his brother Clifford. Sir Arnold says in his recollections, *Farewell My Youth*, that the Baxes came of old Surrey stock and were among the earliest followers of Penn, the Quaker. He admitted that he reflected 'with a certain fat and snobbish complacency' on the fact that his ancestor bought Ockley Court in 1692, and was for a short time Lord of the Manor there.

The garden of Kitlands was open to the public when Mr and Mrs Campbell were living there, but since they sold the house the garden has been closed, which matters less as a large part can be seen without trespassing. It is of special interest because it was landscaped by Sir William and Sir Joseph Hooker of Kew Gardens. There are some very beautiful and rare plants and trees in the garden. By the kindness of Mrs Campbell, I have a copy of the notes she and her husband prepared on Kitlands and its history. Kitlands takes its name from Kitbrook, the stream flowing through the grounds, which is the chief source of the River Arun. The earliest known record is in the Dorking Court Rolls of 1437. It was a substantial farmhouse which changed hands a good many times before it was acquired by the Bax family. It was purchased in 1824 by George Heath, and remained in his family for some 130 years, during which time it was greatly extended. It was during their era that the garden was laid out.

Douglas Denon Heath, who inherited Kitlands from his father in 1852, was a distinguished classical scholar and mathematician. While he was living at Kitlands he was visited by Tennyson, Spedding and the Master of Trinity, who enjoyed discussing philosophy and poetry in the beautiful garden, in which Marianne North painted for Kew 'at least one flower that she had missed in its native Himalayas'. Heath was a generous benefactor to the parish of Coldharbour, and one of the founders and patrons of the Surrey County School at Cranleigh. He was buried in Coldharbour churchyard in 1897. His younger brother was Admiral Sir Leopold George Heath, of Anstie Grange, Holmwood, who took part in the bombardment of Sebastopol and other engagements.

On leaving Kitlands it is possible to circle Anstiebury, crowned by its Iron Age camp, which covers 11½ acres with its double entrenchments, now buried in the woods above the road, and so to circle round to Coldharbour village, 750 feet above sea level. It is small and still quite unspoiled.

19 (opposite) *The barn and pond at Buckland*

The Wedgwoods bought Leith Hill Place, on the southern slopes of Leith Hill, in 1847, and their close relatives, the Darwins, including the great Charles Darwin, frequently stayed there. Ralph and his elder brother, Hervey, and his sister Margaret, spent their happy childhood there. Hervey, who inherited Leith Hill Place, died in 1944, leaving it to Ralph, who gave it to the National Trust. The house is not open to the public.

The Leith Hill range is the eastern outpost of the western Weald, where sandstone and chert overlie the Wealden clay, giving rise to an almost startlingly sudden change of scenery. Here pasturelands and mixed woodlands give way to hills covered with pinewoods, deep valleys and stretches of heathland, of which the highest points are Leith Hill, Hindhead and Blackdown.

Leith Hill, which rises to 965 feet, is the highest summit in south-eastern England, and is easily distinguished by the eighteenth-century tower, the top of which is exactly 1,000 feet above sea level. Leith Hill has its devotees, and any sunny summer week-end will see little family parties, or lone ramblers climbing through the pine-woods, yet it has never had the overwhelming popularity of Box Hill. There is no road to the summit, only trackways, and it is devoid of any attraction but that of its glorious views, which range over the greater part of Surrey and far into Sussex and Hampshire. Aubrey estimated it as a circumference of 200 miles; some have claimed to see even farther, but it is a view which is different on every visit, depending entirely on the visibility. Only in thick mist or heavy rain or a snow storm can it fail to reveal some new beauty never noticed before, and it never stales. The summit, and many acres of the surrounding woods and commons are in the care of the National Trust.

North of Leith Hill, a turning off the Wotton road gives access to the most secluded and unspoiled beauty spot of the area—perhaps in all Surrey—adorable Friday Street. Little has changed since Eric Parker described it in the early years of this century. Two or three houses and an inn huddle together without intruding into the perfect picture of the still surface of the small tarn, which reflects the pinewoods growing down to the water's edge.

Abinger, on a road farther west, has a church, manor-house and an

20 (opposite) *Looking towards the windmill on Reigate Heath*

inn standing beside a small green, well apart from the houses scattered on the slopes of the surrounding hills. It is astonishing to find that this small, secluded church was bombed during the Second World War. It was restored in 1950, but had the further misfortune of damage by fire, which necessitated another restoration in 1964.

North-west of the church, in the garden of Abinger manor-house, which was originally built by Sir John Evelyn towards the end of the seventeenth century, is a small Norman motte. When excavated, it showed that the castle had been a wooden structure, as many of the smaller Norman castles were. Between the manor-house and the church is the manorial pound, which has been scheduled as an Ancient Monument, and in a adjoining field is a mesolithic pit dwelling, excavated by Dr Leakey, which was inhabited by people of the Horsham culture about 5000 BC. The garden is open to the public on a Sunday in June under the Gardens scheme.

There are magnificent beechwoods around Abinger.

Fulvens Farm, dating from the mid-sixteenth century, is one of the best of its kind in Surrey, and Sutton Place Farm has a garden which is also open to the public once or twice in June each year. These farms and some old cottages are at Felday, the hamlet now in the parish of Holmbury St Mary, on the Horsham road (B2126). G. E. Street, who lived at Holmdale, which he had built in 1873, took a leading part in the formation of the parish, for which he built St Mary's Church at his own expense in 1877, two years before his death. He also gave the altar cross of Limoges enamel, and some paintings and carvings from Italy. His second wife, who died in 1876, is buried in a canopied tomb on the outside wall.

Hurtwood Common, which stretches westward from Holmbury St Mary, derives its name from 'hurts', the local name for whortleberries or bilberries. Public access to Hurtwood Common, one of the largest and wildest open spaces near London, was granted by the lord of the manor in 1926.

South of Holmbury St Mary is Holmbury Hill, which has an Iron-Age encampment on its summit, and fine views of the North and South Downs.

Ewhurst, on the A2127, has a church with a massive early twelfth-century nave and some fifteenth-century details, a Jacobean pulpit, and late seventeenth-century altar rails with recessed curved corners and twisted balusters, originally at Baynards Park. There are some old cottages, and a scattering of interesting country houses, very hard to find. Long Copse, built in 1879 by Alfred Russell of the Art Workers' Guild, was thought by G. F. Watts to be 'the most beautiful house in Surrey'.

The Bull Inn, where Cobbett 'treated my horse to some oats and myself to a rasher of bacon' before going on to Ockley, is now a private house.

A road runs north to Peaslake, passing Rapsley Farm, where the foundations of a second-century Roman villa have been found.

Peaslake is rapidly becoming urbanized, but there is a nucleus of stone and tile-hung houses. It is one of several places in Surrey where Sir Adrian Boult lived for a time. He tells in his autobiography, *My Own Trumpet*, how he collected a number of BBC conductors for a week in two successive summers at his 'country bolt-hole at Peaslake' to discuss the art of conducting.

South-west of Ewhurst is Cranleigh, which is trembling on the brink of becoming a town, and fighting strenuously to remain a village, even if one of the largest villages in England—and maintain a village way of life.

Cranleigh's station was closed under the Beeching axe, but that has not prevented Cranleigh from continuing to expand, and it is not surprising that Frank Swinnerton, who has lived there for close on half a century, heads the last chapter of his *Reflections from a Village* with the ominous title 'Passing of a Village'. Yet the village green remains a focal point, with attractive houses of many periods around its edge, including the three Elizabethan cottages made into Old Tokenfield, which the nonagenarian novelist has made his home.

The handsome church of St Nicholas dates almost entirely from the early fourteenth century, with a massive tower and a spacious interior, but had to be restored after damage caused by a bomb in 1944. The font, screen and pulpit date from the fourteenth century, and there is a late sixteenth-century lectern and some monuments of the Waller family. Cranleigh likes to think that the carved head of a cat on the south transept arch gave Lewis Carroll the inspiration for the Cheshire cat in *Alice in Wonderland*.

Cranleigh had the first cottage hospital in England. It was opened in 1859.

Cranleigh School was founded in 1865 for the education of farmers' sons, with only 26 pupils, but was recognized as a public school in 1898, and greatly enlarged the following year. It retains an interest in agriculture, and has its own farm. It also engages in community activities, and in the 1930s the boys undertook excavations in a field where Roman tiles had been found. They discovered about 60 feet of Roman paving and a well-preserved furnace.

South-east of Cranleigh is Vachery, with one of the largest lakes in Surrey, much beloved by anglers, and Baynards Park, which was built by Sir George More of Loseley towards the end of the sixteenth century.

Cranleigh lies on the eastern edge of the 'Fold Country', where the scenery is more like that of the eastern Weald, with copses of oak and hazel, rich pastures, a network of winding streams, wandering roads and secluded villages.

Alford, on the B2133, is almost on the Sussex border. The picture made by the approach to the church is an artist's dream. The narrow path from the main road is flanked by three tile-hung houses of perfect proportions, with the village stocks beside the entrance to the churchyard, and all presided over by the thirteenth-century church with roofs of Horsham slate and a low spire. There is a Jacobean pulpit with its sounding board, decorated with carving in low relief, and an impressive early Norman font, carved with circular-headed arches, each with a Maltese cross on it.

There is a very ancient yew tree in the churchyard, claimed to date from the pre-Christian era, and a much worn slab of Sussex marble, said to mark the grave of Jean Carré, who died in 1572, and was one of the last French glass-makers of the Fold country. He had obtained a licence in 1567 to manufacture 'glass for glazing such as is made in France, Burgundy and Lorraine'. All three of the 'Fold' villages seem to have been engaged in the glass-making industry.

Dunsfold's church is half a mile from the village, on a low hill, a site explained by one of the innumerable legends that all attempts to build it elsewhere were thwarted by fairies or supernatural powers.

As it is just above a holy well with a reputation for the cure of eye afflictions, on the banks of a tributary of the River Arun, it has been conjectured the church may occupy the site of a pre-Christian temple. This village church, dating from around 1270, in spite of the addition of some later details, remains much as it was when built, even to the massive oak pews, some of which were installed when the church was first built. They must be among the oldest in England.

The rectory, east of the church, has a fifteenth-century timber frame, and there are other medieval and Tudor houses nearby or scattered over the parish.

The well is reached by a footpath near the church. A shrine was erected over it by the Dunsfold Amateur Dramatic Society in 1933.

Dr Joseph Warton was born in the Old Rectory when his maternal grandfather, the Rev. Joseph Richardson, was the vicar. Warton was headmaster of Winchester College, and a friend of Dr Johnson. On one occasion when the formidable Johnson told Warton he was not used to contradiction, Warton had the temerity to retort that it would be better if he were!

Chiddingfold is by far the largest and best known of the Fold villages. It has an enormous village green, a pond, a fourteenth-century inn and other ancient inns and houses.

It is still one of the largest parishes in England, but must have had an even greater importance in earlier centuries. A map dated 1556, painted on the wall of the Guarda roba in the Palazzo Vecchio in Florence shows it was the only place in Surrey considered worthy of mention besides Guildford!

Records show that glass was made at Chiddingfold at least as early as 1225, and it was also engaged in charcoal-burning and iron-making. Like all the Fold villages, it had an active smuggling trade, not only in wines and spirits, but in cloth. During the Middle Ages, cloth was legally confined to the towns, but was manufactured in many of these cottages. All these industries have passed away, but it still has a small factory for the manufacture of walking and umbrella sticks, established over a century ago, for which ash plants are specially raised in the parish.

One of the old glass-works of Chiddingfold has been reproduced in the Haslemere Educational Museum. By the thirteenth century

Chiddingfold was the chief glass-making centre in the country, and supplied some of the glass for Westminster Abbey, but appears to have declined at the end of the fifteenth century, when 11 glass furnaces were suppressed as a nuisance, on a petition from the villagers, and only revived for a while in the sixteenth century.

St Mary's Church has some impressive thirteenth-century work, despite the Victorian restoration, when most of the woodwork was swept away, leaving only three exceptionally fine seventeenth-century chairs. One of these is said to have been given to the church by Archbishop Laud when his nephew, Dr Layfield, was rector. Layfield was ejected by the Puritans in 1642, and had to pay a large fine to avoid being sold as a slave, but was reinstated at the Restoration. Among other notable incumbents was Dr Tighe, one of the translators of the Authorized Version of the Bible, who is buried in the chapel.

It is due to the researches of the Rev. Stephen Cooper, a former curate, and his family that some 427 fragments of original Chiddingfold glass were found on the sites of three separate glass furnaces, ranging in date from 1325 to the late sixteenth century. They have been leaded together in a lancet window in the east wall of the church and dedicated to the glass-makers of Chiddingfold, some of whom are named. These fragments, and a few in the Crown Inn, are all that remain of the once-famous Chiddingfold glass.

The Crown Inn has been considerably enlarged and altered since the early years of this century when Hugh Thomson drew it for Eric Parker's *Highways and Byways in Surrey*, and several of the treasures Parker mentions are no longer there, but it is still unmistakably an ancient inn, incorporating genuine fifteen-century work with the splendid original panelling, and possibly even earlier work. During the discreet modernization in 1951, a half-timbered façade was discovered and restored to its original appearance of the sixteenth century.

It is said that Edward VI stayed in the inn in 1552, with his attendants camping on the green. The Crown today is well able to serve a meal 'fit for a king'—for those able to pay for it.

CHAPTER EIGHT

In and Around Guildford

Guildford High Street is so busy with traffic and thronged with shoppers that it is hard to realize there has been an even busier by-pass since 1934, until it is remembered that nearly every major road and railway line in Surrey converges on the town.

With so much activity, the wonder is that the High Street has retained so many ancient buildings, and so much of the charm which inspired Dickens to call it 'the most beautiful High Street in England'. It curves steeply down to the River Wey, and still gives a fine view of the green slopes of Guildown beyond.

Holy Trinity Church, at the top of High Street, was rebuilt in the first half of the eighteenth century, but has a chantry founded in 1540, and some interesting monuments, including the effigy of George Abbot, Archbishop of Canterbury, who founded the Abbot Hospital on the opposite side of the street. The mellow brick building dates from 1619, and is still in use for its original purposes of alms-houses. The Archbishop was one of the six sons of a Guildford cloth merchant. His elder brother, Robert, became Bishop of Salisbury, and his youngest brother, Maurice, was one of the original directors of the East India Company and Lord Mayor of London.

The Archbishop had the misfortune to kill a keeper accidentally when out shooting in 1621. In spite of his known uprightness of character and benevolent disposition, and the fact that he immediately granted an annuity to the widow—who promptly married again—he was much criticized, and bishops refused to be conse-crated by a man 'with blood on his hands'. He fasted every Tues-day for the remaining 12 years of his life, but never recovered his spirits. Charles Kingsley, describing the incident after visiting Bramshill Park, where it occurred, said he had seen 'the very tree where an ancestor of mine, Archbishop Abbot, shot a keeper by mistake'.

St Mary's Church, halfway down the High Street, has a tower of Saxon and Norman work. It was rebuilt in 1180, with alterations in the thirteenth century, and has one of the most attractive interiors in Surrey.

St Nicholas's Church, down by the river, was almost entirely rebuilt in the nineteenth century, but retains the fifteenth-century Loseley chapel, with monuments to the Mores of Loseley House.

The Royal Grammar School was built round a quadrangle between 1557 and 1566. It has one of the five chained libraries in England, given in 1573 by Bishop Parkhurst, who had been a scholar at the school.

The earliest known mention of the game of cricket occurs in a lawsuit brought in 1598, concerning the proposed development of land near the top of North Street, when a witness recalled that 40 years previously he and other boys of the Free School (as it was then called) 'did runne and play there at cricket'.

The superb front of the Guildhall, with its bell-turret, elegant balcony and much photographed clock dates from 1683, but the main structure is Tudor. The Corporation plate includes a rare fifteenth-century mace, traditionally presented to the borough by Henry VII, and a full set of standard measures, presented to the town by Elizabeth I. There are portraits by Lely, and by John Russell, who was a native of Guildford, a scholar at the Grammar School, and four times Mayor of Guildford. He was one of the founder members of the Royal Academy.

An old custom is observed at the Guildhall annually on or about 27 January, under the will of John How, ratified in 1674, by which 'two poor servant maids of good report', providing they do not live 'in any inn or alehouse', throw dice for the interest on £400.

Among a number of other fine old buildings surviving in the High Street is Guildford House, built in 1660. It was the home of the Martyr family, who were known as 'the hereditary Town Clerks of Guildford'. It is now used for Art Shows and other cultural activities. There are also interesting old houses and quaint alley-ways in the adjoining streets.

Guildford was an important coaching centre for travellers between London and Portsmouth, and all the visiting topographers and diarists seem to have carried away happy impressions of the town and its inns. In May 1813, Jane Austen wrote to her sister Cassandra, telling her she and her companions stopped in Guildford for 'a long companionable breakfast'. They afterwards strolled about the town and 'From some views which the stroll gave us, I think most highly of the situation of Guildford.' She visited a shop where she 'was very lucky in her gloves', getting a pair she thought looked 'very well' for four shillings. Unfortunately, she does not mention where they breakfasted, and her admirers of the present day can only hope it was at the Angel, whose hospitable doors are still open to travellers, and not the Lion, which was demolished in 1957.

Guildford Castle was founded in Saxon times, and saw many royal visitors, but little fighting. Only the Norman keep and Castle Arch remain. Nearby is The Chestnuts, marked by a plaque, which was the home of Lewis Carroll's sisters for many years. He died there in 1898, and is buried in Guildford cemetery. The house is not open to the public. South Hill Cottage, overlooking the castle, was the retirement home of Richard Oastler, the 'Factory King' and philanthropist, who compaigned with Lord Shaftesbury for the better condition of children in factories. The Museum of the Surrey Archaeological Society, which has a comprehensive collection of relics of Guildford's long history, is in Quarry Street.

The Corporation has done its part in preserving the atmosphere of Guildford by careful planning, and by persuading shopkeepers not to indulge in neon signs or unsightly developments. The Corporation also provided the island site on the River Wey, at a peppercorn rent, for the Yvonne Arnaud Theatre, which was built by public subscription and opened in 1965.

There are a number of other interesting buildings, old and new, beside the towpath running under great beech trees to St Catherine's Hill. Tudor Braboeuf Manor, on Guildown, is now part of the Law Society's College of Law. At the foot of the hill is a group of carefully restored Cromwellian cottages.

When Guildford was created a separate diocese in 1927, Harold Greig was installed as the first bishop in the parish church of Holy

Trinity, which became the Bishop's Cathedral, but it proved too small. Lord Onslow gave six acres of land on the crest of Stag Hill in 1928, and Edward Maufe, the architect, began work on the site in June 1935. Work was held up during the war, but the building was completed and consecrated in 1961. George Reindorp was the last bishop enthroned in Holy Trinity, and it was the first episcopal enthronement televised in England.

Like so many modern buildings, the interior of Guildford Cathedral is far more attractive than the exterior. The austere lines give an added sense of height, and the light flooding in from the many tall windows adds a feeling of spaciousness and freedom.

The idea of building the Cathedral and University in close proximity is an admirable one, but it is a pity the buildings of the 'technico-logically orientated' university have been allowed to climb so high up the hill that they obscure the dignity of the cathedral from some points of view. Work began on the University in 1966, and the first students moved in 18 months later. It received a Royal Charter in September 1966. Within three years the lively and enterprising students had launched the Guildford Festival, and they continue to play their part in the life of the town.

The origin of the name of Guildford would seem self-evident, but as it is clear no guild existed in the town until centuries after the name was first recorded in the will of King Alfred as 'Guldeford', several other origins have been propounded and hotly disputed—which only goes to show the perilous paths trodden by dedicated etymologists! According to Malory, the town 'which is now in English called Guildford' was Astolat, home of Elaine, the fair maid who died of love for Sir Lancelot.

South of Guildford there are some of the most interesting and unspoiled places in Surrey, scattered over the whole area between the pine covered hills of the Weald around Hindhead and the open Weald of the 'Fold' villages. Three main roads give access to the network of lanes—the most easterly is the A281 through Shalford, the A3100 runs south-west through Godalming to Haslemere, and the A3 through Milford to Hindhead.

Those who hurry through Shalford may possibly notice the trim cottages, the church and the inn with the unusual sign of a sea-horse, but they can have no conception of the peaceful charm of the eighteenth-century water-mill beside the Tillingbourne, which is still the most attractive of small rivers near its confluence with the River Wey. The mill is one of the most interesting in Surrey. It belonged originally to the Godwin-Austen family, and was a working corn-mill until 1914. Major Arthur Godwin-Austen gave the mill to Ferguson's Gang, which has been called a 'saintly mafia'. The members are elected by secret ballot and are known by pseudonyms. They swear to follow the leader, Ferguson, in preserving England, and have made repeated gifts to the National Trust from 1930 onwards. They presented Shalford Mill to the Trust in 1932. The members are drawn from all over England and do not confine their work to Surrey. Their masked leader made a broadcast from Broadcasting House in 1935, as a result of which 600 new members were enrolled and £900 contributed. Thousands of pounds have been raised by the Gang, whose anonymity is still preserved.

Most of the machinery of Shalford Mill remains intact, but the storage area has been converted into a house, the charming garden of which adds to the attractions of this rural nook of Shalford.

The Victorian church has a Tudor brass, and eighteenth-century tablets to the memory of the Austen family, including Col. Haversham Godwin-Austen, explorer and geologist, who won the Founder's Medal of the Royal Geographical Society for his exploration and survey of the north-west Himalayas. He died in 1923. His father, Robert Alfred Cloyne Godwin-Austen, was an eminent geologist.

One of the Vicars of Shalford was the Rev. David Hamilton, who served as a chaplain in France, and afterwards conceived the idea for the tomb of an Unknown Warrior, which was taken up by the Dean of Westminster.

South-east of Shalford is Great Tangley, perhaps the finest half-timbered, moated house in Surrey. The earlier hall-type house was adapted and enlarged in 1584, and has some later additions.

South of Great Tangley is Wonersh, which has known many variations in the spelling of its name, one of which was 'Wogeners'. It has always appealed to visitors with its well-cared for street of half-timbered houses, its church of many periods since the Saxon era, and its fifteenth- and sixteenth-century brasses. The church is set beside a green presented to the village in 1935. The sixteenth-century inn, The Grantley Arms, takes its name from the Grantley family, whose seat, Wonersh Park, was demolished in 1935. The Hon. George Norton, Recorder of Guildford, brother of the third Lord Grantley, married one of the three beautiful grand-daughters of Sheridan, better known as the poetess Mrs Norton, who suffered much from her husband's cruelty.

Still farther south along the same road (B2128) is Shamley Green, delightfully grouped around a large green cut into unequal triangles by the road. There are a number of attractive old cottages with which, so far, modern developments have blended well.

Godalming, four miles south of Guildford, has been saved by the by-pass which carries the road to Portsmouth well to the west of the town. It has a remarkable number of delightful old houses, some with medieval wattle and daub, and overhanging upper storeys. The King's Arms, although it bears the date 1753, has much earlier timberwork and panelling. Peter the Great, Czar of Russia, and his suite stayed there in 1698, and consumed a gargantuan meal, the bill for which is preserved in the Bodleian Library.

Among visitors to the White Hart (formerly The Antelope) were Sir Francis Drake, Admiral Lord Nelson, and Tomochichi, a Red Indian chief, brought there by General Oglethorpe to lunch with other Indians.

Godalming has shown admirable restraint in adjusting to modern traffic needs, even to the extent of an ingenious adaptation of Crown Court, and the retention of its Old Town Hall, the most conspicuous and characteristic building in the High Street. In spite of its name, it dates only from 1814, but stands on the site of the medieval market. The Council Chamber is now a museum worthy to rank among the most interesting in Surrey, largely through the comprehensive collection of Surrey by-gones made by Gertrude Jekyll, who lived at Munstead nearby. She gives an account of the customs, trade and agriculture of the district in *Old West Surrey*.

The restored church is especially remarkable for its tall thirteenth-century spire—a rarity in this area. The church has some pre-Conquest and Norman work, two sixteenth-century brasses and interesting murals. The Rev. Samuel Speed, grandson of John Speed the famous map-maker, was Vicar in the seventeenth century.

The Rev. Owen Manning, who was Vicar for 37 years, began the great *History of Surrey*, which he had to relinquish when he became blind five years before his death in 1801. It was completed by William Bray of Shere. The churchyard slopes down to the River Wey, and on the north side is the Phillips Memorial Cloister by Thackeray Turner, commemorating the heroic chief wireless operator, a Farncombe man, who went down in the ill-fated *Titanic*. The planting was planned by Gertrude Jekyll, who also designed the garden of the local Police Station.

Among other residents of Godalming were Sir Theophilus Ogle-thorpe, who led a charge against Monmouth at Sedgemoor, and bought the manor of Westbrook in 1688, and his son, General James Edward Oglethorpe, who founded the State of Georgia, USA, and was a great prison reformer. Westbrook House has since been rebuilt.

Arthur Clutton-Brock the critic, essayist and journalist, who died in 1924, and Philip Heseltine, who edited Elizabethan music and wrote on Delius and other musical subjects under his own name, and composed songs and chamber music under the pseudonym Peter Warlock, are both buried in the cemetery, half way between God-alming and Farncombe.

Famous in her day was Mary Tofts, wife of a clothworker, who claimed to have been frightened by a rabbit in 1726, when she was pregnant, as a result of which she gave birth to a stream of rabbits. Several celebrated physicians professed to believe her story and published pamphlets about the phenomenon. Hogarth satirized the event, and there was a prodigious uproar until Queen Caroline sent her own doctor to investigate, and exposed the racket. Mary Tofts was sent to Bridewell.

Prominent on a hill above the town is Charterhouse School, originally founded in London in 1611 as a boys' school and a hospital for aged men. The school removed to Godalming in 1872. The roll-call of Old Carthusians includes Richard Crashaw, Sir Richard Lovelace, Roger Williams, founder of Rhode Island, USA, Addison, Steele, John Wesley, W. M. Thackeray and after the school moved to Surrey, Lord Baden-Powell, founder of the Boy Scout movement, Ralph Vaughan-Williams and Sir Max Beerbohm.

Among the relics preserved in the library are the *Epigrammata Sacra* of 1634, said to be the first book published by an Old Carthusian; Leech's drawings for his *Comic History of England*; part of Thackeray's MS of *The Newcomes* and collections of letters of some of the more famous Old Carthusians.

Aldous Huxley, the novelist, was born in Peperharow Road, on the south of the school grounds, when his father was a Housemaster at Charterhouse.

Godalming was a royal borough in Saxon times, and after the Conquest had a long association with the diocese of Salisbury. Its prosperity was founded on the wool trade, and as early as the twelfth century it developed its cloth trade, under the influence of the Flemish immigrants who came to England in the reign of Henry 1. When the wool industry of other West Surrey towns began to decline, Godalming's clothing industry continued to flourish, and some of the cloth manufactured there was exported to the Canary Islands. It also had two or three paper-mills and three corn-mills.

The coaching era, the extension of the Wey Navigation Canal to Godalming in 1754, the establishment of a knitting industry and the coming of the railway, each in their turn added to the prosperity of Godalming. Traffic fell away in the 1930s, when the by-pass was constructed, but has returned in such volume in recent years that there was ominous talk of an inner relief road which would have involved the demolition of the most attractive houses in Godalming. This proposal was opposed by the more far-seeing people of Godalming, supported enthusiastically by the Governor and people of the State of Georgia, who feel a proprietory interest in the town from which their founder came. Now various traffic detours have been arranged and so far the threat to Godalming has been averted.

A mile west of Godalming is the hamlet of Eashing, where a short road runs down from the Guildford by-pass (A3) to the medieval bridge across the River Wey. This noted beauty spot is now in the care of the National Trust.

A mile south of Godalming is Munstead, where there are many notable country houses in the thickly wooded hills, most of which were built by Sir Edwin Lutyens, with the encouragement of Miss Jekyll, who laid out many of the gardens. He built Munstead Wood for her after the death of her mother, Mrs Julia Jekyll. It was here this remarkable woman lived for 35 years, pouring out a stream of articles and books promulgating her ideas on gardening, inspired by William Robinson, who had first opposed the stiff Victorian bedding-out.

As a girl she had trained as an artist, and when failing eyesight forced her to give up her career, she brought her feeling for colour and design into the planning of her garden at Munstead Wood, and in gardens in all parts of the British Isles. She also had adherents on the Continent and in the Americas. Nothing was too small or too large for her to undertake, and she gave as much care and thought when writing to a young factory worker in Rochdale who had advertised asking for advice on the planting of his window box, as to designing the planting schemes for the British Cemeteries for the Imperial War Graves Commission after the First World War.

Among her earlier friends were Mary Severn (sister of Arthur Severn, the friend of Keats) Brabazon, Ruskin and other artists, and in later life all the best-known horticulturalists of the day visited her garden at Munstead Wood.

Miss Jekyll also learned wood carving from the village carpenter and silverwork from an Italian craftsman in Italy. Works by her were bought by the Museum of Science and Art, and other museums.

Gertrude Jekyll died in 1932, at the age of 89, and is buried in the churchyard of St John the Baptist, Busbridge (now within the boundaries of Godalming). Her books are still quoted in gardening books, articles and broadcasts, and her ideas are still the guiding principle of the gardens of this and many other countries.

Winkworth Arboretum, farther south along the B2130, covers nearly a hundred acres of lakes and hillside planted with rare trees and shrubs. The Arboretum is open freely to the public, but never seems to attract too large numbers of visitors at any time of the year. It is an almost unbelievably peaceful refuge from the rush of modern life, now in the care of the National Trust.

Farther south still is Hascombe, sheltering under Hascombe Hill, which is crowned by an Iron-Age camp. Hascombe is almost entirely laid out as an estate of 'gentlemen's residences', a number of which were designed by Lutyens in his earlier years. High Leybourne, a tile-hung house, was the work of Lutyen's builder, Thomas Underwood, for Archibald Thorburn, the painter of birds and animals. Thorburn's *British Birds*, illustrated with 192 plates in colour, ran into many editions, and his other classic, Thorburn's *Mammals*, has been republished recently. He also painted the annual Christmas card for the Royal Society for the Protection of Birds until his death at High Leybourne in 1935.

The spirited prancing White Horse sign Miss Jekyll painted in 1926 for the inn beside the main road was removed in the early 1960s.

Hascombe Hill is the most easterly of the three which form a triangle round the north of the Fold country. The second is Hydon Ball which with Hydon Heath was given to the National Trust in 1913 as a memorial to Octavia Hill, one of the founders of the Trust. The hill was planted and paths laid out by local troops of Boy Scouts under the direction of Miss Jekyll.

The third hill is Hambledon, with the village scattered over the slopes and the Victorian church on the summit.

It is only a short distance from Hambledon to Witley Station, just west of the A283, near which is the handsome building housing the King Edward's School. It was founded in London as a result of a sermon by Bishop Ridley in 1552, and removed to Witley in 1867. The Rev. A. C. B. Bellerby, who was Headmaster from 1926 to 1961, was an outstanding sportsman who had represented England at the Olympic Games. He gave a greater impetus to sports at the school, but also increased its scholastic stature. He kept its traditions alive during the period of the Second World War, when the school was evacuated to the Institution at Hambledon, to enable the Admiralty to occupy the spacious premises at Witley. A plaque presented by the Admiralty records that it was here naval radar was developed for use in the Battle of the Atlantic and other naval operations. The school is now co-educational.

Witley is a typical Surrey village of the most attractive kind. The ancient church has an elaborate thirteenth-century font, a sixteenth-century brass and twelfth-century wall paintings growing ever less distinct with the passing years. Timbered houses and cottages and a medieval rectory are grouped around, and the White Hart Inn has an inglenook known as 'George Eliot's Corner'. She and G. H. Lewes bought The Heights at Witley as their country home about 1876.

Witley Park, originally Lea House, was built in 1890 by the financier Whitaker Wright, who was an amateur landscape gardener, and built, among other things, a fantastic room beneath the lower lake in the gardens, with a gigantic statue of Neptune rising from the roof above the water of the lake. The house has been demolished.

Witley Court (originally The Hill) was built in 1861 for the painter, Birket Foster, to his own design. This also has been demolished, with the exception of some outbuildings. The Burne-Jones windows and a tile overmantel are in the William Morris Museum at Walthamstow. Both Birket Foster and Whitaker Wright are buried in the churchyard.

Witley is surrounded by wide commons and woodlands, many of which are owned by the National Trust, which is establishing a Visitors' Centre on Witley Common with exhibits explaining management problems in the preservation of the countryside; a Conference Room; and a Laboratory. Lectures will be given by the Warden and Nature Trails arranged. Visitors, and especially teachers with parties of school children, will be welcomed. It is hoped to have the Centre open by the Autumn of 1975.

The modern highway to Portsmouth (A3) skirts the western side of Stag Hill at Guildford, and passes close to the site of a Roman village on the way to Compton, south of the Hog's Back and close to the Old Road. Compton is a very pleasant village in a well-wooded country, famous for its eleventh-century church of St Nicholas, and its many associations with the painter, G. F. Watts. The church has curious Romanesque additions made in the twelfth century to the chancel, including a two-storied sanctuary which is a unique survival, the reason for which continues to baffle even experts in church architecture. The upper storey is open to the chancel, but is protected by a balustrade of Norman woodwork believed to be the oldest of its kind in England.

Limnerslease was designed for Watts in 1891, and his wife designed the red brick cemetery chapel in 1896, in the form of a Greek cross. The elaborate symbolic interior decorations arouse admiration or horror according to the taste of the visitor. Watts is buried in the cemetery in a cloister designed by Mrs Watts in a vaguely Moorish style. The Watts Gallery was opened in 1904, the year in which Watts died, and has a representative collection of his wide range of paintings. It is in the grounds of the Potters' Guild started by Mrs Watts, and some of the tiles made by the villagers can be seen surrounding the door of the chapel.

Gilbert White is so identified with Selborne that it is often forgotten he spent the first ten formative years of his life at Compton.

West of Compton is magnificent Loseley House, built in a beautiful park in 1562 by Sir George More, an ancestor of the present owner, with stones brought from the ruins of Waverley Abbey. It has remained almost unaltered since it was first built, and has much of its original furniture. It also has splendid panelling, plaster ceilings, a magnificent mantelpiece of chalk said to be the work of Holbein, tapestries and needlework.

The Mores were a very distinguished family, high in royal favour, and the Loseley Papers are a valuable source of information, especially on the Tudor period. Elizabeth I was entertained there three times, James I and his Queen twice, and the late Queen Mary stayed there in 1932. It has also been used as the background for five films and on TV. It is open to the public on several afternoons each week in summer.

About a mile and a half north of Eashing a turning on the west of the A3 leads to Shackleford, a pleasant mixture of old cottages and modern houses in the centre of a sparsely inhabited parish which includes the village of Peper Harow.

The Midletons became lords of the manor of Peper Harow in 1719, and kept the hamlet thoroughly rural by a benevolent despotism. Park House is in a noble park of over 350 acres laid out by 'Capability' Brown. It was built in the eighteenth century and given an additional storey in 1913. Among those entertained there by the first Earl of Midleton were Curzon, Balfour and Churchill.

After the Earl's death in 1942, it was turned into a school, and the whole estate was broken up—chiefly into large-scale farms.

Peper Harow Farm has an immense seventeenth-century barn on wooden staddles, and is one of the finest in Surrey. It should not be confused with Oxenford Grange, in the south-west of the Park, which was built by Pugin in 1843 in medieval style. Oxenford was originally the property of Waverley Abbey, and later the site of the original Peper Harow House.

The heavily restored church of St Nicholas has some Norman work, a Victorian arcade of Irish marble from the Midleton quarries in Co. Cork, and some interesting memorials, including a fifteenth-century brass to Joan Adderley, widow of William Brocas, Lord of Peper Harow; a seventeenth-century brass to Sir Thomas Broderick and his wife, and an effigy of the fourth Viscount Midleton, who died in 1836.

Peper Harow ('heag' or temple) is one of several villages in the neighbourhood with names said to be derived from the Norse for a holy place or god. Another is Thursley ('Thor's or Thunor's field'), ome miles to the south-east.

Thursley was once a centre of the Surrey iron industry and the pits from which the iron ore was extracted can be seen on Thursley Common.

The restored church has much Saxon work and a thirteenth-century chapel with massive beams and arches resting on four extraordinary corner posts or tree trunks 2 ft. 6 in. thick. Faint traces of an eleventh-century wall painting were discovered in 1927, and there is one of the rare survivals of an oven recess for baking the wafers used in the Mass. The Norman font is a magnificent Bargate stone tub. Some fifteenth-century Flemish glass was brought from Costessey, Norfolk.

In the churchyard is the much-visited grave of an unknown sailor murdered in 1786 by three men he had treated to a drink. Their foul deed is also commemorated on a stone on Gibbet Hill, where they were hanged.

Not far from the sailor's grave lies John Freeman, the poet and critic, who died in 1929 when not quite 50 years of age. His work was valued by contemporary poets and writers, and won him the Hawthornden Prize in 1920, but was undervalued by the general public. His best-known prose work is *Portrait of George Moore*. He was also an excellent man of business, and rose from a junior clerk in the Liverpool Victoria Friendly Society to become Secretary and Director within the space of 24 years, and the efficient organizer of a staff of over 7,000. His *Last Poems* were published in 1930 with an introduction by J. C. Squire, and his *Letters* were edited by his widow and Sir John Squire.

Freeman was a great lover of the countryside, in which he wished to be buried, and the site looking out over Crooksbury Hill was chosen for his grave. In 1931 eight acres were bought as a memorial to him, to protect the view, and were given to the National Trust.

Although only half a mile from the busy A3, Thursley is one of the outstandingly beautiful villages of this part of Surrey, with a splendid view of Hog's Back from the village street, which is full of delightful houses, with some fine unrestored old cottages contrasting with good examples of Lutyens' work. Lutyens grew up in Thursley at The Cottage (now Lutyens House), and his mother and his nephew Derek are buried in the churchyard.

North of Guildford, Worplesdon borders the A322, with the older nucleus scattered around a village green, and St Mary's Church well placed above it. The church has a fine Perpendicular tower and thirteenth-century work, but has been much restored. There are some memorial tablets and fragments of fifteenth-century stained glass, but of greater interest is a small window with a portrait of the Rev. Duncan Tovey, Rector of Worplesdon, who died in 1912. He was an authority on the poet Thomas Gray, whose works and letters he edited. Still better known is his younger son, Sir Donald Tovey, musical scholar, pianist, composer, lecturer and broadcaster. Donald Tovey began studying the piano with Miss Weiss at Northlands, Englefield Green, and spent his holidays at Worplesdon, before his appointment as Reid Professor of Music in Edinburgh, where he established the Reid Orchestral Concerts in 1917. Among his many friends were Joachim, Adila and Jelly d'Aranyi, and Pablo Casals.

He was a learned and witty writer and lecturer, and added much to the prestige of English musical scholarship.

Merrist Wood, on the south-west of Worplesdon, was built by

Norman Shaw in 1877, on a beautiful site looking towards the Hog's Back. It has been an Agricultural College since 1945.

The name of Worplesdon, derived from Waple, a raised pathway, and dun, or hill, denotes a place of very ancient origin, and traces of prehistoric settlements have been found on the breezy, heathery commons by which it is surrounded—commons which merge into the area on the west and north which is now almost entirely devoted to army manoeuvres.

The A322 continues north to the crossroads where the B380 turns off on the east to Woking and on the west to Pirbright, in the heart of the military area, but still clinging to reminders of its past in the White Hart and Cricketers' Inns, fine houses around the large green, and mansions in the neighbourhood. Henley Park, a much-restored eighteenth-century house, is on the site of the mansion of the Earl of Essex, the too ambitious favourite of Elizabeth I. The church was rebuilt in 1783, and has late Victorian work at the east end. Its chief attraction is the grave of Sir Henry Morton Stanley, the Welsh journalist and explorer, who found Livingstone. He bought the estate of Furze Hill six years before his death, and is buried in St Michael's churchyard. A granite monolith bears the inscription 'Henry Morton Stanley, 1841–1904', with his African name, Bula Matari, and the word 'Africa'.

The main road (A322) continues north past the enormous and magnificently landscaped Brookwood cemetery, which was founded in 1854. Various areas have been allotted to London parishes and communities such as the Chelsea Pensioners, the Corps of Commissioners, Oddfellows, the Actors' Acre and others, but it is perhaps best known for its American Military Cemetery, dedicated to the memory of 540 United States soldiers and sailors who died in England during the First World War, who are buried in an area which is owned by the United States Government. It adjoins the British Military Cemetery and the Canadian War Memorial building.

Farther north again the A322 passes through Knaphill, an infelicitous modern development, to Bisley, which is best known for the annual rifle-shooting competitions for the King's Cup and other major trophies. The great Common was enclosed for the National

Rifle Association in 1890, in succession to the camp at Wimbledon. Bisley's ancient church, set in fields apart from the village, is worth more than a passing glance, and nearby is St John the Baptist's Well, mentioned by Aubrey, the water of which was formerly used for baptisms.

Beyond Bisley the A319 turns east to Chobham and the A322 bends north-west across Bagshot Heath to Bagshot, which is now part of the great military complex spilling over the Surrey border into Berkshire.

Chobham, a most attractive village, is especially notable in an area which has not usually developed so happily. There are numerous old inns, houses and farms, presided over by the handsome church of St Lawrence, which dates back to the eleventh century, with fifteenth- and sixteenth-century details, including unique elbow beams in the Lady Chapel. Although over restored, it still has the massive pillars of a Norman arcade; a wooden porch said, on doubtful authority, to have come from Chertsey Abbey at the Dissolution; a large iron-bound chest with three locks, dating from the thirteenth century, and a wooden sixteenth-century font. New oak pews have been given by members of the congregation as thank offerings or memorials, to replace the hideous Victorian pews, and the wrought-iron lighting brackets were made in 1951 in the local forge.

Included in the list of Vicars is the Rev. Thomas Taunton, who was Vicar from 1595 to 1652, and is said to have been 117 years of age when he died.

There are several early nineteenth-century monuments, and a memorial to Nicholas Heath, who was deprived of his office as Bishop of Worcester by Edward vi, and again as Archbishop of York and Lord Chancellor when Elizabeth i came to the throne. He was sent to the Tower, but Elizabeth treated him leniently, 'believing his mistaken Piety sincere'.

The name of Bee Farm, on Chobham Common, is a reminder that it was not until 1215 that the parishioners obtained from Pope Honorius the right to bury their dead in the churchyard, instead of having to take them to Chertsey Abbey—and were made to pay 20s. and supply 10 pounds of beeswax annually for the privilege!

Precious Farm marks the site of a great pond made by the monks of Chertsey Abbey, which became choked with weeds a century after it was described by Aubrey.

An obelisk on Chobham Common commemorates a review of the troops by Queen Victoria in 1893, which was the forerunner of the Army's occupation of so much of the West Surrey border. Curiously enough, they subsequently made little use of Chobham Common, which is still a fine expanse of open land, in spite of the encroachment of the M3, which cuts right across it.

CHAPTER NINE

Farnham, Hindhead and Haslemere

The road between Guildford and Farnham runs along the Hog's Back, where the North Downs narrow until in some places there is barely enough width to accommodate the modern highways, and it has been badly affected by the increase in traffic since the 1960s.

The A31 follows the line of the Neolithic Old Hoar Way, with the Old Road or Pilgrim's Way and the new North Downs Way on the southern slopes. There are glorious views south across the wooded hill country to the Sussex border, and north across the rich pastoral landscape, which looks in the distance much as it did in Cobbett's day, with the ugly sprawl of the modern towns along the Blackwater River fortunately invisible.

There are three charming and unspoiled villages on or close to the Old Road. Compton has already been mentioned. Puttenham, the second village, can be reached by a road which drops steeply down from the A31. It is on the dividing line between the chalk and sand, and the cottages are on a slope which necessitates outside steps to some of them, as at Old Oxted. There are also some fine old houses, and although the church has been badly restored, it still has a Norman arcade and windows, an early eleventh-century tower, and a brass to Edward Cranford, in priest's vestments. He was rector from 1400 to 1431. Henry Beedell was rector for 38 years, his son, also Henry, was rector for 56 years and their successor, Thomas Swift, for 59 years—the three between them spanning the reigns from Elizabeth I to George II.

Many insights into the history of the older houses and of village tragedies and scandals are given in a history compiled by the Puttenham and Wanborough Local History Group. Between Puttenham and Seale is Shoelands, a charming old house now chiefly of seventeenth-century work, but with an older core. The manor was held by Selbourne Priory in the thirteenth century for an annual rent of a golden spur.

Seale's over-restored church has a few survivals, including an attractive fourteenth-century timber porch, and brasses from the graves of the Woodroffes of Poyle Manor, north of Hog's Back, including Sir Nicholas, who died in 1578, and his wife, Grissel. There is a white marble mural to a young officer, drowned with other members of his regiment, on the way to join the British forces in Spain in 1809, the incident being shown in relief beneath the inscription.

Many versions of the origin of the name of Seale exist, mostly derived from Saxon words meaning willow, or a hall or building, or an area dedicated to a Saxon god.

In Norman times most of Seale was included in the manor of Tongham, on the northern side of the Hog's Back, and today they are linked in the ecclesiastical parish of Seale with Tongham.

Tongham, less fortunate than Seale, has been swamped with modern dwellings, due to its proximity to Aldershot, and Poyle manor-house has been demolished. There are still some old houses and farms to be found, but on the whole it is more rewarding to visit Wanborough, where the thirteenth-century church of St Bartholomew claims to be the smallest in Surrey. It consists of a single cell measuring only 45 × 18 ft., which was used as a granary and also as a carpenter's workshop from 1674 until its careful restoration in 1861. It is dwarfed by the magnificent tithe barn—some 95 × 30 ft.—which dates from the second half of the fourteenth century. The manor-house beside the church has the date 1527 on it, but was built in the seventeenth century.

Wanborough is one of the all too few places in Surrey which claims to have a gastronomic 'speciality'—Wanborough Lardies—a recipe for which was contributed by Mrs Frank Ackerman to *Country Fare*, prepared by the National Federation of Women's Institutes for the *Daily Mail* Ideal Home Exhibition in 1954.

North of Wanborough is the place-name Christmaspie, but I have been unable to discover any special recipe with which it is associated, although it is thought the name may refer to a feudal rent payable to the abbots of Waverley, who owned the land. It is on the outskirts of Flexford, which was originally little more than a single seventeenth-century house, but is now a rash of new houses spreading north to Wanborough Station.

Normandy, just over two miles north on the A232, is chiefly noted for its association with William Cobbett, who bought the little Normandy Farm shortly before his last illness. It was there the grand old controversialist died peacefully in the summer of 1835.

North of Normandy are the vast Commons marked on the map as 'Danger Areas', where army manoeuvres are carried out, and west is Aldershot, the most southerly of the long line of towns strung out along the main roads of the Hampshire–Berkshire border in a seemingly unending succession for many miles without a break.

Aldershot and Farnborough are Hampshire towns which are beginning to spread over into Surrey, but Camberley, Frimley and Bagshot, close to the Berkshire border, are wholly in Surrey. Although the greater part of the National Army Museum has been removed from Camberley to London, the Indian Army Collection is still to be seen in the beautiful Regency buildings of the Royal Military Academy, which is set in a large park. It is hoped the former Irish Army collection will be opened to the public there in 1975, and there is a small Cadet Collection in the Sandhurst Museum nearby.

Francis Brett Harte, better known as the American poet and short-story writer, Bret Harte, died at Red House, Camberley, in 1902. His tales of the Californian gold rush, particularly *The Luck of Roaring Camp and other Sketches*, published in 1870, achieved enormous success. He is buried on the north side of Frimley churchyard, under a stone with the inscription 'Death shall reap the braver harvest'. Also buried at Frimley is Admiral Frederick Charles Doveton Sturdee, of Falkland Islands fame, who died in 1925.

Frimley, with a history dating back to prehistoric times, is also developing rapidly, but still has a few old houses at Frimley Green.

Bagshot's Victorian church has memorials to members of the royal family given by the Duke of Connaught, who lived at Bagshot Park, said to be the last house built by Benjamin Ferrey, on the site of a hunting seat of James I and Charles I. Pennyhill Park, built in 1873 on a hill in a splendidly landscaped garden, is now an hotel.

Bagshot Heath, covering the infertile Bagshot Sands with acres of heathland, was the horror of our ancestors, who had no love of natural scenery, and hated wild places for their barrenness and their danger from highwaymen, who infested such areas. Many tales are told of their depredations, and they are featured in Gay's *Beggar's Opera* and Smollett's *Roderick Random.* Defoe called the Heath 'Not only good for little but good for nothing'.

Between the wars, it was still possible to see something of the haunting beauty, and experience the feeling of loneliness and wide horizons on Bagshot Heath, but with the progress of the M3 churning up so much of what is left by the encroachment of housing needs, it is now a mere wraith of its former size and fascination. Yet, even here, there are some compensations still. No part of Surrey has more extensive nurseries, where rhododendrons, azaleas and evergreens are cultivated and exported all over the world. Some of them have played a leading part in pioneering the growing and hybridization of many new species from the Himalayas and Western China. There are also large areas of woodlands and pastures, all along the road to Staines (A30), as a reminder that this area was once a part of Windsor Forest.

Farnham, beautifully set in the narrow valley of the Wey close to the Hampshire border, is the only town actually on the Old Road or 'Pilgrims' Way', which here joins the Hoar, or 'Harrow' Way, and is now Farnham High Street.

Inevitably, fine old buildings have disappeared since the coming of the railway, yet much remains, and the town has contrived to keep the atmosphere of a small market town, as befits the birthplace and last resting place of William Cobbett. It has a by-pass which takes much of the through traffic, and although it has reached out to engulf such villages as Bourne and Wrecclesham, the country comes so close that there are cobbled passages leading into the main road, and field paths converging on the A31.

Castle Street is so short and slopes so gently up to the castle that it is amusing to find Fanny Burney complaining, when she visited Farnham in 1791, that she was 'ready to fall . . . from only ascending the slope to reach the castle', and could not climb to the top of the keep to see the glorious view. Castle Street is almost entirely

Georgian, apart from the delightful row of almshouses dating from 1619.

The red-brick castle, half-hidden in trees, was built by Bishop Henry of Blois, brother of King Stephen, and was a palace of the bishops of Winchester until the diocese of Guildford was formed in 1927, and a seat of the bishops of Guildford until 1956.

Like Guildford and Reigate Castles, it was captured by the Dauphin in 1216, but it also played a part in the Civil War, even if it was an ignominious one. Two poets held it alternately—the Parliamentarian, George Wither, who surrendered to Prince Rupert, and the royalist Sir John Denham, who surrendered to Sir William Waller. All but the sixteenth-century gatehouse was so thoroughly dismantled that it cost Bishop Duppa, the first bishop after the Restoration, over £2,000 to make it habitable, and his successor, Bishop Morley, spent another £10,000 on repairs which were severely criticized by Aubrey for their 'lack of regard to the rules of architecture'.

Most of the English monarchs from Edward 1 to Queen Victoria were entertained in the castle, but it is the bishops who have left outstanding memories there. Bishop Morley, although the most hospitable of men, was an ascetic, who slept in a cell-like room on a stone bed, ate only one full meal a day, never warmed himself at a fire, and never married, but lived to the age of 86. When he became bishop he invited his life-long friend, Izaak Walton, to live with him. Walton frequently stayed in the room allotted to him, and wrote his *Lives* of Hooker and Herbert there—doubtless refreshing his spirit at intervals by fishing in the River Wey.

Bishop Thorold, who repaired the roof of the castle, also laid 'one mile and 100 yards of stair-carpet', and Bishop Sumner, who occupied the See for 42 years from 1827, laid out the garden.

Edna Lyall (Ada Ellen Bayly), the Victorian novelist, who spent much of her childhood at the home of her relatives in West Street, laid the scene of two of her novels in Farnham, and has left a delightful pen-picture of Bishop Sumner shortly before his death: '. . . he sat in his carriage watching a Punch and Judy show in the park, given to the parish school children, and I can still see his dear laughing old face and real enjoyment of the fun'.

Bishop Sumner used to drive to outlying churches in his diocese to preach, without giving warning of his coming. On one occasion the old churchwarden hurried down to the carriage and said 'M'lard, we can't let 'ee preach this afternoon, 'cause a stranger's agoin' to, but you can read a lesson if you like.' It says much for the bishop that he always enjoyed telling the joke against himself.

The castle is now a Centre for International Briefing, and is open to the public at advertised times. The magnificent deer park, which was for centuries a jealously preserved hunting ground, is open freely to everyone.

The Castle Theatre was a small eighteenth-century barn off Castle Street, adapted for use by a repertory company which gave performances there from 1939 until the company removed in 1974 to the fine new Redgrave Theatre, on an excellent site leased to the Farnham Repertory Theatre Trust by the Council, who also contributed £7,800 towards the cost.

The centre of the long main street is The Borough, which is extended by East and West Streets. West Street, with its handsome Georgian houses, is the more obviously rewarding, but it pays to explore all Farnham's streets for their quaint alley-ways. Vernon House, where Charles I spent a night as a prisoner on his way to his trial and execution has a seventeenth-century core. It is now the Public Library. Willmer House, now the Museum, has much beautiful furniture and a wealth of relics of Farnham's long history.

Winkworth Place is typical of the little courtyards which survive in Farnham to delight the investigator, the most notable of which are the spacious cobbled courtyard of the skilfully modernized Bush Hotel, which Thackeray mentions in *The Virginians*; and the narrow Lion and Lamb courtyard overlooked by half-timbered houses.

Much of the conservation in Farnham is due to the public spirit of the townsfolk. Splendid work has been done by the Farnham Building Preservation Trust, formed in October 1968, which has rescued a number of the older buildings and preserved the exterior while modernizing the interior. The eighteenth-century Maltings beside the Wey, which continued in use until 1955, was bought by the townspeople, and The Maltings Association was formed as a charitable Trust to hold the freehold on behalf of the town. The buildings are to be preserved and turned to many useful purposes. The Surrey Community Development Trust has also helped in the work of preserving and converting old houses in Farnham.

The Jolly Farmers Inn, an attractive seventeenth-century brick building in Bridge Square, in which Cobbett was born, has been renamed The William Cobbett.

The parish church is chiefly of fifteenth-century work, although it incorporates some twelfth-century details, but has been so drastically restored that only the sunshine flooding in through the windows relieves it from a feeling of bareness. Among the numerous monuments are some worn brasses, a monument by Westmacott, and a long eulogy in memory of the Rev. Francis Toplady, remembered now only for his hymn *Rock of Ages*. He was born in West Street, in a house which has since been demolished.

There is also a medallion portrait of William Cobbett, erected by 'his colleague in Parliament' John Fielden, whose name is carved as prominently as that of Cobbett. Eric Gill has carved a statue of St Andrew, to whom the church is dedicated, and a short inscription in modern lettering to George Sturt, who was born in The Borough, and wrote under the pen-name of George Bourne. We shall meet him again in Bourne. Both Cobbett and Sturt are buried in the churchyard, but Toplady was buried in London.

The church has a painting by Stephen Elmer, ARA, who was born in Farnham, and died unmarried in 1796. Gilbert White, in *The Natural History of Selborne* (Letter 9 to Thomas Pennant), refers to 'Mr. Elmer, the celebrated game painter at Farnham', and the *Dictionary of National Biography* says: '. . . he developed a special power in depicting still life and dead game, and was perhaps the most successful painter in this line that England has produced'. Unfortunately he was not so successful in figure painting. His portrayal of *The Last Supper*, originally over the altar, was removed to the tower, and when it was discovered in 1963 that it had been tacked on the back of the *Tables of the Decalogue*, it suffered the ignominious fate of being re-hung with its face to the wall!

Farnham was formerly a great centre for pottery, and much of the green and blue Farnham Ware was exported to London, where in Elizabethan times the pots were 'usually drunk in by gentlemen of the Temple'. An account of these earlier potters and potteries is given by George Sturt in his book about his grandfather, *William Smith, Potter and Farmer, 1790–1858*. The only old-established pottery still surviving is at Wrecclesham, now a suburb of Farnham, where Absalom Harris, whose mother was a niece of William Cobbett, and was descended from a long line of potters, removed in 1872.

Encouraged by Birket Foster, the painter, and with the assistance of W. H. Allen, Art Master at the Farnham School of Art, Absalom developed a flourishing trade in a new Farnham Green Ware, which was sold at Liberty's, Heal's, and other London shops, before the Second World War. Staff shortages, and other difficulties, and finally, the impossibility of obtaining an essential ingredient of the Farnham Green Ware glaze led to its discontinuance. Examples of pots believed to have been made originally in Farnham in earlier times are to be seen in the Victoria and Albert Museum, and the Farnham Museum has specimens of the newer Farnham Green Ware.

The Wrecclesham pottery is still carried on by Absalom's grandsons, Arthur and Reginald Harris. The family home adjoins the potteries, and by the kindness of Mr Arthur Harris I saw the vast stores of horticultural wares in which the firm now specializes, and which are exported to many parts of the world.

South of Farnham is Bourne, now also within the boundaries of Farnham. Vine Cottage, Lower Bourne, was the home of George Sturt and his sisters after he retired in 1891 from the wheelwright's shop he had inherited, to devote himself to writing. *The Wheelwright's Shop* is usually hailed as his masterpiece, but he himself thought his *Journals* were his most valuable writing. More widely popular are his descriptions of Farnham in *A Small Boy in the Sixties*, for which his friend Arnold Bennett wrote a long introduction, his various memoirs of his family, and above all the 'Bettesworth' books published under his pen-name of George Bourne, in which he records conversations with his gardener, whose real name was Frederick Grover. Grover, industrious, loyal and with a rough kindliness, was bitterly contemptuous of wastrels, and at times given to insensitive practical jokes and 'orkardness', but was at all times worthy of respect for his sturdy independence.

Anyone who wishes to know the true life of the Surrey countryside and its labourers in the nineteenth century cannot hope to find them better described than in the Bettesworth books, with their lucid, beautifully balanced prose. They have a unique value as a reflection of an age that has passed for ever, described with an understanding and lack of sentimentality rare at that period. They depict poverty in all its grimness, underlining the necessity for change, but leaving room for regret that so much of the independence, the humour and capacity for the enjoyment of small pleasures seems to have been lost in the process.

Nearby in Vicarage Lane is the house where Marion Cran (Mrs George Cran) lived, and where she created a garden from three acres of heathland and pinewoods. In *The Garden of Ignorance*, first published in 1912, she tells of her abysmal ignorance in those early days. Her style of writing is very different from that of George Sturt, and is sometimes jarringly whimsical, but when these lapses can be overlooked, the book is outstanding in its encouragement for the novice. She afterwards bought Coggers, near Benenden in Kent, and described her work of restoration there in *The Story of My Ruin*. She died in 1947, and Mr Christopher Neve, the present owner of Coggers, tells me admirers of her books still come to see the house, including some of the rising generation, as interest in her work has been re-awakened. She was a popular lecturer and broadcaster, and contributed Gardening Notes to *The Lady*.

Just across the Hampshire border from Farnham are The Wakes, Selborne, home of Gilbert White, and Jane Austen's home at Chawton, both of which are open to the public. Sherlock Holmes is remembered in Aldershot, in Farnham itself, and in the neighbourhood of Crooksbury Hill; Nicholas Nickleby and Smike at Hindhead, and many another real or fictional celebrity in this lovely south-west corner of Surrey.

East and south of Farnham the north branch of the River Wey pursues its erratic course to Tilford, past Moor Park, for ever associated with the memory of Sir William Temple and his wife, Dorothy Osborne, whose love letters during their long and seemingly hopeless courtship are some of the best known in the English language, and with Sir William's secretary, Swift, and Esther Johnson, his beloved 'Stella'. The house appears to date from the eighteenth century but encases the seventeenth-century house bought by Sir William. It is now a college for adult education.

Close beside another bend in the Wey are the ruins of Waverley Abbey, in the shelter of Crooksbury Hill. The Abbey was founded in 1128 by William Giffard, second Bishop of Winchester, but was so constantly damaged by floods that the church was not dedicated until 1278. Nicholas de Ely, then Bishop of Winchester, feasted all comers for nine days at his own expense to mark the occasion, and it is said 7,000 guests sat down to meat on the first day alone. Even as it had been the first Cistercian Abbey to be founded in England, so it was one of the first of the smaller monasteries to be dissolved. Sir William More took many wagon loads of stone from the abbey to build his grand new mansion of Loseley, and people were still quarrying in the ruins at the end of the nineteenth century, consequently the ruins are not extensive. Part of one transept, most of the cellarium and one end of the monks' dorter remain, and the whole of the ground plan has been recovered by excavation. It is now in the care of the Department of the Environment, but has remained closed 'for repairs' for the last year or two. The Department informs me it is not possible to give a date when it will re-open, which may not be for two or three more years.

It is believed Walter Scott took the name of the abbey for his Waverley novels, but more intimately associated with it are the opening chapters of Conan Doyle's *Sir Nigel*, which depicts the struggle of local landowners against the rapacity of the abbots, who employed the most cunning legal devices to secure the lands of their less well-briefed neighbours.

The Milford Road (B3001) runs south-east from Waverley to Elstead, where there is a medieval bridge, a sixteenth-century timber-framed farm-house and a small triangular green. The church is much restored, but has fragments of medieval work, including some massive timbering in the roof and porch, and a ladder up to the belfry consisting of a single oak plank with notches for steps. Elstead Mill is of eighteenth-century work with a Tudor core. It may well stand on the site of a mill for which the miller was paying dues to the Bishop of Winchester in 1208. An iron fire-back in a Tudor fireplace of the mill-house has a royal coat of arms supported by the lion of England and the Red Dragon of Wales, surmounted by a Tudor crown.

The Woolpack and The Golden Fleece inns are a reminder that in earlier times Elstead was a centre for the processing of wool. It became known later for the manufacture of braid.

Elstead is surrounded by sandy commons, and a group of three Bronze-Age barrows has been discovered on Turner's Hill, Crooksbury Common.

The five-arched Somerset Bridge, north-east of the village on the road to Peper Harow, may mark Sumaeres Ford, which was mentioned in a charter of AD 909.

There are two roads from Farnham to Hindhead, the more easterly of which is the Tilford Road, which passes the wood in which lies Black Lake on which J. M. Barrie centred the Never Never Land of *Peter Pan*, and which was also the background for *Dear Brutus*.

He used the now much altered Black Lake Cottage as his country home from 1900 to 1909. It was here he held a Cricket Week annually with his famous amateur cricket team. He explains in *The Greenwood Hat* how the team was named the Allahakbarries from a combination of his own name and the Arabic for 'Heaven help us', which was very appropriate for a team which played with hilarious incompetence, enjoying themselves enormously and even managing to win on occasion.

The northern branch of the Wey is joined by the southern branch at Tilford, which has two medieval bridges, a very large green celebrated in cricketing annals, a famous oak tree beside the Barley Mow, the eighteenth-century Tilford House, and pleasant modern houses half-hidden in trees.

Tilford was the home of Nigel Loring, hero of Conan Doyle's historical novel Sir Nigel, and it was at one of Tilford's bridges that he barred the way on his great horse, Pommers, in his makeshift armour, challenging the knights in the train of Edward III to 'some small deed of honour', with ludicrous results.

Tilford achieved a wider renown in 1953 with the first concert of the Tilford Bach Festival, arranged by Denys Darlow, the distinguished conductor, organist, broadcaster and Bach enthusiast, then organist of Tilford Church. He was backed by a committee of local residents, and the concert aroused such enthusiastic support that the Tilford Bach Society was formed to promote an annual Festival of the music of J. S. Bach, and of his 'predecessors, contemporaries and successors, in a manner most consistent with the style and demands of the period'.

Performances have been kept at the highest possible musical standards, and soloists of international fame are engaged. The Festival was broadcast 'live' by the BBC, and soon the Tilford Bach Festival Choir and Orchestra were in demand not only locally but in the principal concert halls of London and the provinces, Westminster Abbey, City churches and various Festivals, and abroad in West Germany, Switzerland, and Belgium. A number of first performances were given as a result of extensive musical research and of works commissioned by the Society. The ever-increasing reputation of the Festival has also resulted in various broadcasts and recordings. An off-shoot of the Festival Choir, the Tilford Festival Ensemble, has made recordings of Bach's *Musical Offering* and *The Art of Fugue*, and Peter Warlock's *The Curlew*.

The appointment of Denys Darlow as organist and choirmaster at St George's, Hanover Square, has provided an additional and much larger venue for a 'Bach in London' Festival which has enabled major works to be performed.

The Tilford Festival Choir and Orchestra also give four concerts a year in Farnham Castle for members and friends.

South of Tilford are the Devil's Jumps, the odd-looking hills associated with legends of the thunder-god Thor and the Devil, and described by Cobbett as 'three rather squat sugar-loaves'. He thought the placing of them so wonderful that he could not believe they were formed by 'mere chance'.

Nearby are the crossroads presided over by The Pride of the Valley Inn, and Stock House Farm, the home and workshop of Mr Christopher Monk. He began making cornetts (wooden instruments which were especially popular in the Renaissance, which must not be confused with modern brass cornets) in 1955, when he found he was

179

unable to buy or commission anyone to make him one with which to play the great range of early music written for the instrument. He began in the workshops of St Edmund's School, near Hindhead, where he was then teaching history and English, and had to evolve his own techniques to solve the many problems in copying sixteenth-century originals. In 1972 he gave up teaching, and devoted himself to the making of cornetts, cornettinos and serpents to meet the rising demand resulting from the present widespread renewal of interest in early music, which he has helped to create.

He carves all the serpents and the best of the cornetts and cornettinos by hand in wood, but also makes cheaper cornetts in resin, by a process devised by Len Ward and his technician Ted Kirby, at Fernhurst. These are particularly appreciated in American schools. The cornettinos are modelled on an original dated 1518; cornettos on a seventeenth-century keyless original; keyless serpents are copied from a Serpent d'Église by Baudouin; and three-keyed serpents from a standard English pattern by Pretty. A considerable percentage of his instruments is exported to all parts of the world, and even behind the Iron Curtain. His wife looks after the bookkeeping and despatch of the instruments.

He is an accomplished musician, able to test all the instruments he makes, and to play the old instruments in his remarkable collection. He is in constant demand at concerts and festivals of early English music, plays regularly for The Churt Consort of Cornetts and Curtals, and the Cornetts and Sackbutts group, and in the works of Maxwell Davies and other *avant-garde* composers who are now writing for the cornett and serpent. He has also played in films, and on radio and TV, and is making records, so far as the ever-increasing demand for his instruments allows the necessary time.

Frensham Common, on the main Hindhead Road (A287) is famous chiefly for the two great ponds now owned by the National Trust. It is difficult now, looking at the peaceful Little Pond, surrounded by pinewoods, or the expanse of the Great Pond with graceful sailing yachts gliding over it, to realize that shortly after the declaration of war in 1939 these lovely lakes were completely drained for fear they would give guidance to enemy aircraft. Trees grew so thickly that many feared the lakes would not be the same again, but today they look as though they had never been disturbed. Best of all, the wonderful wild-life of the area has remained faithful to its haunts. From White of Selborne onwards, observers have recorded rare birds in the neighbourhood, and it was here Julian Huxley first watched the courtship of the great crested grebe.

Frensham church was mentioned in the records of Waverley Abbey, when it was moved from its original site in 1239, but the Victorian restoration left little of interest apart from the Perpendicular tower, and the great copper cauldron known as Mother Ludlam's. She lived in a cave at Moor Park, and was apparently of a benevolent disposition, for she was generous in lending the cauldron to her neighbours, but is said to have taken umbrage when a borrower failed to return it promptly, and abandoned it—which sounds as highly improbable as Aubrey's story that it was brought by fairies, who used it for their feasts. Much more likely is the tradition that it was 'filled to the brim' with ale at village weddings, and probably for wassailing and other village festivals.

Beyond Frensham Great Pond the road climbs steeply to Churt, where David Lloyd George, first Lord Dwyfor, farmed and carried out agricultural experiments during his retirement.

Climbing up past the golf course, it is only two miles to Hindhead crossroads, where the shops and cafés along the Portsmouth Road are in sharp and unwelcome contrast with the pinewoods and heather-clad heights of Hindhead, Gibbet Hill and the deep valley of the Devil's Punch Bowl. Hidden away in the pinewoods are the houses where so many celebrities lived in the nineteenth century that to list them all would be like reciting from the pages of *Who's Who*. One of the first of these was the distinguished natural philosopher, Professor John Tyndall. He built Hindhead House in 1885 as a 'retreat for his old age', and spent the greater part of the last years of his life there. He is buried at Haslemere.

In 1898, shortly after George Bernard Shaw's marriage, he and his wife rented Blencathra (now a school) on the London–Portsmouth road. He declared the air there made him feel 'a new man', and although he spent some time in 1900 at Blackdown Cottage near Haslemere, writing the Preface and Notes for *Three Plays for Puritans*, and the following year was at Piccards Cottage, St Catherine's,

Guildford, they did not leave Blencathra for Hertfordshire until 1904.

Arthur Conan Doyle bought a plot of land opposite the Royal Huts Hotel at Hindhead in 1895, on the advice of Grant Allen, who believed the air of Hindhead would suit Doyle's consumptive first wife as well as that of Switzerland. Undershaw was built to his own design.

Doyle was knighted in 1902, and appointed Deputy Lieutenant of Surrey. With the encouragement of Lord Roberts, he formed at Undershaw the first of the rifle clubs which afterwards spread all over the country.

On the death of Lady Doyle in 1906, Sir Arthur sold Undershaw and moved to Sussex. The house is now a private hotel.

Hindhead reaches 895 ft. at Gibbet Hill, the second highest point in Surrey. The ground falls steeply eastward, and the flanks are scored by steep-sided valleys, of which the Punch Bowl is un- questionably the most striking. There are many greater heights which command less extensive views than Gibbet Hill. On the east is the Weald, dominated by Leith Hill; north are the long line of the Downs and the far-reaching commons of the heath country; and west and south the whole sweep of the South Downs—range after range of hills constantly changing as the visibility varies, but always arrestingly beautiful.

In spite of the enormous crowds at week-ends, there is no wilder scenery in the south of England than the view across the Devil's Punch Bowl, or Haccombe (Highcombe) Bottom. It was here the Broom Squires of Baring-Gould's novel lived in cottages on the slopes of the Punch Bowl. Baring-Gould caught the wild and lonely beauty of the Punch Bowl in his day, but it was Kingsley in *My Winter Garden* who gave the best description of the wild, free men who were 'the descendants of many generations of broom squires and deer stealers'. Eric Parker met some of them in 1908, but even then they were a disappearing race, whose cottages were in ruins.

It was on Gibbet Hill the three murderers of the sailor buried at Thursley were hanged in chains, in 1786, on the old road skirting the Devil's Punch Bowl. The memorial stone records the fact, and gives an account of the fate of the assassins, which was listened to by

Smike with 'greedy interest' when Nicholas Nickleby read it to him on the way to Portsmouth. The chains in which they were hanged are preserved in the Royal Huts Hotel, together with a series of crude paintings illustrating the murder.

Haslemere, three miles south-east of Hindhead, was once a rotten borough returning two members to Parliament—which roused Cobbett to the peak of invective! Today it is one of the most attractive places in Surrey. It owes the preservation of its charm, and the beauty of its surroundings, to the people who settled there in the nineteenth century, rather than to the indigenous Surrey folk, some of whom, indeed, would have exploited it mercilessly for building sites.

When Sir Robert Hunter settled at Haslemere in 1881, he was already known for his successful work for the Commons Preservation Society, and in 1895 he became one of the three founders of the National Trust. He led the fight for the preservation of the natural beauty of Surrey, and today the Trust owns over 2,000 acres in the neighbourhood of Haslemere and Hindhead alone. So many and so varied are its properties all over Surrey—as elsewhere—that it has not been possible to mention more than a tithe of them, and the reader who is interested must be referred to the list issued annually by the Trust.

After Sir Robert's death at Haslemere in 1913, Waggoners' Wells, a series of ponds set among woodlands, just over the Hampshire border, was bought as a National Memorial to him.

Arnold Dolmetsch, who settled in Haslemere during the First World War, made the name of Haslemere a household word to lovers of music all over the world. Here he revived the playing of fifteenth- to eighteenth-century music, training every member of his family to make and play the necessary instruments, establishing workshops, publishing books on the interpretation of old music and founding the annual Haslemere Festival. The Dolmetsch Foundation was established in 1928 at the instigation of leading musicians, men of letters, businessmen and politicians, to ensure the continuation of Dolmetsch's immense programme of activities.

'Factory' is a misnomer for the large and airy premises where almost everything is done by hand. The workshops are open to the public on Thursdays, and it is fascinating to watch the care with which harpsichords, clavichords, viols, recorders and other instruments are made, and valuable old instruments, including violins fragile with age, are being repaired. It is heartening in these days of mass production to see the dedication of all the craftsmen, and the number of enthusiastic young apprentices who can be trusted to carry on the Dolmetsch tradition of perfection.

The Festival, founded in 1925, and the workshops are now directed by Arnold Dolmetsch's son, Carl Frederick Dolmetsch. He, too, is an authority on early music and instruments, and has given recitals in all parts of the world.

The High Street of Haslemere, with its many half-timbered and Georgian houses and its picturesque old Town Hall, is always a delight. Pollarded limes screen some of the shop fronts, and a magnificent chestnut tree, planted in 1792, stands beside the Georgian Hotel. Farther up is the sixteenth-century burgage house, with its handsome Georgian front, which houses the Haslemere Educational Museum—another rather misleadingly intimidating name for a most fascinating record of history, with particular reference to local life. It had its origin in 1888, when Sir Jonathan Hutchinson, an eminent surgeon who had given much thought to museum reform, set up a small private museum on novel lines at his home, Inval. After his death in 1913 the museum was carried on by a local committee under the Chairmanship of the distinguished geologist, Sir Archibald Geikie. It removed to its present site in 1926, and incorporated the Peasant Arts Collections previously in Foundry Road. *The Times* rightly described the museum as 'a pioneer and pattern among country town museums'. Every item is related to its background, and there is a 'Space-for-time' display of geological succession which always has a crowd of deeply interested youngsters studying every section. Adults and children can also take part in practical field studies in the laboratories and the extensive grounds and adjoining National Trust lands, with the help of experienced demonstrators.

St Bartholomew's Church was rebuilt in the nineteenth century, with the exception of the thirteenth-century tower. It has a window designed by Burne-Jones to the memory of Tennyson, who lived at

Aldworth House on Blackdown, just over the Sussex border. Among the many other celebrities who have lived in or around Haslemere are Josiah Wood Whymper, the water-colour artist and engraver, and his son Edward Whymper, the famous mountaineer, who lived at Town House in the High Street; Sir Francis Galton, founder of the School of Eugenics, who died at Grayshott House; Sir Arthur Wing Pinero, the dramatist; George Macdonald, the poet and novelist, and George Eliot, who wrote most of *Middlemarch* in a cottage on Shottermill Common.

Haslemere is so close to the Hampshire and Sussex borders that it can be made a touring centre for these counties, but there is so much to be seen in West Surrey that there is scarcely any need to go farther afield.

Index

*The numerals in **bold** type refer to the figure numbers of the illustrations.*

Index